What people are saying about "Predictable Revenue"...

"Reading *Predictable Revenue* is like having a delicious conversation with a sales guru who generously shares his sales process, results and lessons learned. I'm so impressed, energized and refreshed to hear such relevance mixed with humor and unabashed logic. This book is honest, relevant and logical and it's rated A++ because it's guaranteed to make you think and convinces you to change things up....fast. Now, please excuse me as I'm running out to a funeral for my phone. After reading my favorite chapter on RIP Cold Calling there's no doubt its dead and gone and Aaron tells us why."

-Josiane Feigon, CEO of TeleSmart and
author of Smart Selling on the Phone and Online

"I just finished reading your book. Unbelievable! I now know what's wrong with our sales process…"

— Pat Shah, CEO, SurchSquad

"I have read Predictable Revenue and it's Entrepreneurial Crack!"

— Damien Stevens, CEO, Servosity

"Working with Aaron Ross has been nothing short of amazing! His methods applied to our sales organization helped us produce a profitable and scalable new stream of predictable revenue. We saw at least 40+% new business growth. The best part is, we had a blast while doing it!"

— Michael Stone, VP Sales and Strategy, WPromote
(#1 ranked Search Marketing Firm on the Inc. 500)

"The concept of the sales machine is brilliant. Aaron has done a great job distilling a complex concept into a simple-to-read, consummate bible for entrepreneurs and executives."

— Promise Phelon, CEO, UpMo

"Aaron has created a work that is useful to established companies and entrepreneurs. The material is easily digested and applicable to businesses large and small."

— Brent Mellow, CEO, akaCRM

"The companies I've seen that have followed Aaron's advice have outperformed. What more can I say?"
— *Tim Connors, General Partner, US Venture Partners*

"Aaron's one of the leading thinkers of the Sales 2.0 movement. I am inspired by Aaron's vision, amazed by his creativity, and thankful for his counsel."
— *Daniel Zamudio, CEO, Playboox*

"Aaron has been a great advisor for AdaptAds. His 'cautiously but surely' approach matches that of AdaptAds. He brings invaluable learning experiences in terms of building a sales team. He's accessible, with the most astute of perspectives."
— *Yogesh Sharma, CEO, AdaptAds*

"Aaron is the quintessential example of how great leaders can be if they set aside their egos, create a clear and bold vision, and empower their people to execute like mini-CEOs. I took over the team that Aaron created at Salesforce.com and I've been amazed by his leadership in building a solid foundation set for explosive and sustainable success. Thanks Aaron. You've made me look mighty good around here!"
— *Ryan Martin, Director of New Business, Salesforce.com*

"Aaron is really unique—on the one hand he is a savvy and experienced businessman, and on the other hand he is a grounded and balanced person who truly enjoys helping others become successful. He's able to think like a bootstrapping entrepreneur and corporate chief at the same time. He knows that yesterday's methods aren't enough to create sustainable and predictable growth in the new economy. It is a real pleasure to know and work with him."
— *Eliot Burdett, Founder and Managing Partner, Peak Sales Recruiting*

"Aaron has an amazing ability to assess, guide, and teach CEOs how to shift their approach to business to help them create more predictable revenue, a sales staff that runs itself as a sales machine, and to reduce stress and increase freedom in their lives. It's been my honor to work with him and witness the changes he helps others bring forth."
— *Onna Young, LifeAfterDebt.us*

"After attending my first CEOFlow Sales Machine gathering, I realized many of us CEOs face remarkably similar core issues. Better yet: the experience and advice from one entrepreneur is incredibly timely and relevant to another. There's nothing better than having a conversation with a group of bright, motivated leaders to focus on what makes a company great."
— *Andrei Stoica, Founder, ConnectAndSell*

"There is something extraordinary that happens when smart business leaders sit down to talk about their ideas for transforming business, and Aaron Ross is a master at guiding these conversations to help find the real gems. I think a best-selling business book could come out of every one of these events—wish I had the time to write one of them."

— John Girard, Founder, Clickability

"Aaron Ross quickly grasped the issues and provided extremely helpful and creative ideas firmly rooted in his expertise about business growth. Most impressively, he did this with sensitivity to my personal motivations and comfort level. Thanks to Aaron, I now feel at ease moving my business to the national level."

— Klia Bassing, CEO, VisitYourself.net

"Aaron is insightful, intelligent, and highly dedicated to the missions he designs for his life. The focus, drive, and determination Aaron demonstrates are admirable qualities that inspire. I would recommend Aaron to any company that is looking for a good person, who is also a strong and formidable leader."

— Kim Santy, Founder, Soul Shui

"Aaron has always looked out for and fought for the best interests of people who work for him. Beyond that, he is smart, strategic, and can go just about anywhere he wants to go in this industry. He's a quality guy who I would jump to work with in the future."

— Brendon Cassidy, VP Sales, EchoSign

"You are doing good helping people Aaron—your work will not go unnoticed. Sharing and helping others is a true talent of yours."

— Ryan Born, CEO, AudioMicro

"As usual, Aaron's inspiring and his innovative Cold Calling 2.0 tactics are refreshing. I love that Aaron makes sure to include helpful advice on how to hire and compensate the best talent for maximum success. You can have great sales tactics and tools, but it will all be wasted if you put the wrong butts in the seats and neglect that talent! Follow Aaron's hiring advice and you'll see great results like I did."

Kevin Gaither, Founder and CEO, InsideSalesRecruiting.com

Predictable Revenue:

Turn Your Business Into A Sales Machine With
The $100 Million Best Practices Of Salesforce.com

Aaron Ross

and

Marylou Tyler

ISBN: 978-0-9843802-1-3

Aaron Ross
PebbleStorm, Inc.
8605 Santa Monica Blvd, #39743
West Hollywood, CA 90069
Contact: info@pebblestorm.com

(310) 751- 0656

www.PredictableRevenue.com
www.UniqueGenius.com
www.PebbleStorm.com
www.CEOFlow.com

Limits of Liability and Disclaimer of Warranty

Warning – Disclaimer

Dedication

Thank you, Rob Acker, Shelly Davenport, Cary Fulbright, Frank Van Veenendaal, Ryan Martin, Marc Benioff, Jim Steele, Brett Queener, RTL, John Somorjai, Erythean Martin, all the past, present, and future members of the Enterprise Business Representative sales teams around the world, and my many other Salesforce.com friends and supporters.

Thank you, Tim Connors, Roberto Angulo, and John Girard, for getting me started on the sales consulting path after Salesforce.com.

Thank you, Jon Miller & Maria Pergolino, for your support with the *Predictable Revenue* book and message.

Thank you Onna Young, you are a genius and very special to me! Who knows what PebbleStorm would be like without you? (Everyone needs an early adopter or first cheerleader, mine was Onna Young.)

Thank you, Marylou Tyler, for helping wildly expand the vision, growth and fun of PredictableRevenue.com, and Kristine Castro Sloane for taking such great care of me, this book and PebbleStorm!

And last and most of all, thank you my wife Jessica Ross, the most loving, honest, authentic and fun woman ever, who unfaillingly believes in me, supports me and helps me grow.

Foreword

It's popular now to believe you can grow a business through values like *purpose, happy employees and customers, vision* and *fulfillment.* They work, as proven by companies like Zappos!

But - "purpose" isn't enough, and if your sales are sucking wind, it's really hard to be happy.

It's all well and good to want to make a big difference, make money, create a fulfilled, happy workforce and change the world... but how are you going to do all that if you are living month-to-month, paycheck-to-paycheck, struggling constantly with your financial goals?

In order to make a difference that sticks, you also need solid, simple and sustainable sales practices.

What if you could implement an enjoyable sales process that can generate a predictable flow of highly qualified sales opportunities, month after month?

What would your company's revenue and growth look like if you could grow new business sales by 40%-300% — without having to make another unproductive cold call ever again?

I wrote this book to help executives and sales organizations feel the success, freedom and peace of mind that come with having predictable revenue.

My Purpose: To Help You Make Money Through Enjoyment

My purpose, which my sales teachings are a part of, is to help you make money through enjoyment (your purpose and passions), so that you can live a free, fun and fulfilled life that combines money and happiness.

An important part of enjoying work in a company, whether you're an executive or an employee, comes from creating predictable income and sales, and freeing yourself and your team from the day-to-day slog of constantly wondering where each new customer will come from.

You Can Make As Much Money As You Want, Doing What You Love

In addition to *Predictable Revenue*, I have two other bodies of work. *Unique Genius* helps you discover your purpose and turn it into a business you love. *CEOFlow* helps you turn your employees into mini-CEOs.

Through mentoring hundreds of people, and from my own experience, I have learned these truths:

1. You can make as much money as you want.
2. You can do anything you love.
3. Your work can fulfill you and make a difference in the world.
4. You can feel powerful, valuable, and capable of making an impact.
5. You can have the peace of mind and freedom that comes with having all the support you want from people that you trust and respect.

You can get a free ebook about this at www.PebbleStorm.com/manifesto.

Above all... jealously guard your enjoyment.

Contents

1

Where the $100 Million Came From

*I'd never done business-to-business sales in my life
before I joined Salesforce.com, which actually helped me create the
breakthroughs I did...*

Start Here

I'm going to start by addressing head-on one of the biggest misconceptions in modern, effective sales: that adding salespeople is what grows revenue.

Do you want the peace of mind that comes with knowing your own sales organization will be a "Sales Machine," cranking out predictable revenue, generating new leads on demand, and meeting your financial goals without your constant focus and attention?

I created a sales lead generation process and team at Salesforce.com that helped increase revenues by more than $100 million in the first few years. Partners and I then taught the same process to other companies, helping them double and triple their new revenue growth, like Responsys (the #1 Saas Marketing Platform), WPromote (the #1 search engine in the Inc 500), and HyperQuality (tripled their results in just 90 days). It's common for 80-95% of our clients' sales pipeline to come from this outbound process, driving the bulk (or all) of their growth.

Of course you want more revenue, but what good is it if it isn't predictable?

Of course you want more revenue, but what good is it if it isn't predictable? One-time revenue spikes that aren't repeatable won't help you achieve consistent year-after-year growth. You want growth that doesn't require guessing, hope and frantic last minute deal hustling every quarter- and year-end.

The book is based on more than eight years of experience at Salesforce.com and consulting and advising dozens of other technology and business services companies including SuccessFactors, Responsys, Servosity, Clickability, AfterCollege, 4INFO, CitrusByte, Savvion, Trulia, WPromote, X1, BrightEdge, NEOGOV, Bovitz Research Group, and others.

Three Keys To Predictable Revenue

Building a Sales Machine that creates ongoing, predictable revenue takes:

1. Predictable Lead Generation, the most important thing for creating predictable revenue.

2. A Sales Development Team that bridges the chasm between

marketing and sales.

3. Consistent Sales Systems, because without consistency you have no predictability.

Both at Salesforce.com and in consulting with companies, I've found time and again that the biggest impact on predictable revenue, the lowest hanging fruit, is made by creating an outbound sales development team that focuses 100% on prospecting (that means no closing deals and no working inbound leads!) You will learn all about what actually works in the "Cold Calling 2.0" sections in this book.

Bite-Sized Chunks

Sometimes all it takes is one good idea, one right practice, to get things moving again. I write this book as a series of bite-sized chunks of ideas that you can scan and try out.

My intention is provide you a resource guide or manual that you can open to any page and find something useful to learn and apply.

Are You New To Sales, Or A New CEO

I wrote the book primarily for people who have some sales experience, so we jump right into topics early in the book like "Fatal Planning Mistakes" and "Cold Calling 2.0."

If you're new to sales, sales management or being a CEO, I'd recommend you first read "Chapter 6: Lead Generation & "Seeds, Nets & Spears", and "Chapter 7: Seven Fatal Sales Mistakes CEOs and Sales VPs Make."

Those two chapters will help give you more of a "Sales 101" foundation before getting into the rest of the book.

The "Hot Coals" Sketch

What CEO or VP Sales doesn't relate to this image? You've all been through, or are feeling now, these "Hot Coals" of stress, missed results, and uncertainty:

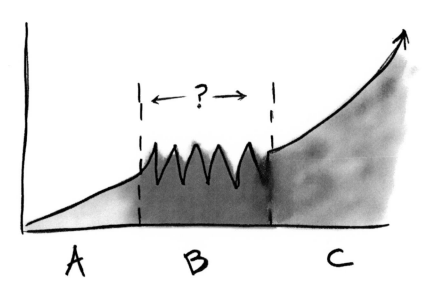

Usually the cause of the "hot coals" is a shift from organic growth "A" (based on getting customers through founders relationships and hustling or organic internet marketing) to proactive growth "C", which is based on investing in programs that generate predictable growth.

Shifting from organic growth to proactive growth requires new habits, practices and systems, causing a lot of delays and frustrations.

Appreciate that the shift is a process which does not happen overnight. Stay committed, persistent, and patient as you get through the "Hot Coals," whether it takes months or--in many cases--years.

My goal for this book is to help you get through the hot coals as quickly, easily and profitably as possible.

That will only happen if the management team and board understand the same fundamental principles around what creates predictable revenue (and it's not about hiring more salespeople).

The Painful Planning Mistake Boards & Sales VPs Make Every Year

Reminder: if you are brand new to selling, I'd recommend starting by reading Chapters 6 and 7.

I'm going to start by addressing head-on one of the biggest misconceptions in modern, effective sales: that adding salespeople and working them harder is what grows revenue.

For companies selling products worth less than $100,000-$250,000, the old school strategy of hiring more "feet on the street" to drive revenue growth is failing more often than not.

Let's take companies who want to grow fast, mostly through adding new customers (rather than more mature companies who drive much of their growth through their customer base).

The problem they face is that the old bedrock sales principles that worked before the Internet do not work anymore. "I need to double revenue growth, and I need to double my sales force to drive it, or make my current team work twice as hard."

Wrong. In high-productivity sales organizations, salespeople do not cause customer acquisition growth, they fulfill it.

This is a huge shift in traditional sales thinking. I'm talking about root cause drivers, not correlations. Of course you need more salespeople if you're getting bigger, but they aren't what is causing the bulk of new customer growth.

Also, while they are quite popular and simple sales strategies of CEOs, sales executives and salespeople, "work harder" and "make more calls" don't scale.

Most salespeople already work enough hours, and trying to get them to work harder is like trying to solve a problem by going faster in the wrong direction. It's bailing water out of the boat faster rather than fixing the leak.

In other words, working harder translated usually means: "what we are doing isn't working, so do more of it!"

Lead Generation Causes New Customer Acquisition

I see a future in which sales is more and more like account management, and the focus of new customer acquisition responsibility growth falls more squarely on lead generation executives with titles like (VP Demand Generation, VP Pipeline Growth, VP Lead Generation, VP Sales Development).

Okay, some of you are saying, "You're crazy. I'm hiring salespeople and they're adding new revenue. And it's worked for me for 10 years. Without great salespeople, we wouldn't be closing these customers."

Right. That did work in the past. Things change.

It's true that you need great salespeople to close customers, but the better your lead generation is, the less dependent you are on the quality of your salespeople and sales process. Better lead generation = more margin for sales error.

Let's do a quick comparison of two competitors:

Competitor A:

- Trying to double from $10 million in revenue to $20 million.
- 10 salespeople today, growing to 15.
- Generating $3 million per month in new pipeline through proven campaigns in lead generation and marketing (40% of pipeline), a Cold Calling 2.0 team (40% of pipeline), and partners (20% of pipeline). [We'll get to what these terms mean later in the book.]
- Their salesperson ramp time is 4 months, because they create pipeline for the rep to "walk into."

Competitor B:

- Trying to double from $10 million in revenue to $20 million.
- 10 salespeople today, growing to 20.
- Competitor B spends money on marketing, and salespeople cold call, but no one really tracks pipeline metrics. But the VP Sales and the salespeople have had a knack for hitting their numbers each month so far (with some scrambling).
- They think their new salesperson ramp time is 3-6 months (but they really will end up at 6-15 months... if their salespeople ramp at all).

Which competitor would you bet will hit their goals?

Here's the scenario I personally see playing out for too many companies in the next 12 months as they plan next year's operational goals and plan:

1. The board and/or CEO set an aggressive revenue target for the coming year (mostly based on new customer acquisition).

2. The Sales VP and/or CEO divides the revenue target by the expected quota of each salesperson to determine the number of salespeople needed to hit the target.

3. It takes longer than expected to hire the new salespeople, and salespeople miss their targets after ramping MUCH more slowly than planned.

4. As the end of the year approaches with a big results gap to make up, everyone has an extra helping of frustration with a side of stress for Thanksgiving.

A Fatal Mistake

The root assumption that gets Sales VPs fired (although the Board and CEO are equally responsible) is the false assumption that salespeople will find new business on their own from past Rolodexes or lots of cold calls, with a minimum of help or investment from the company.

They won't generate enough leads on their own... at least not enough to feed themselves. (Okay, sometimes, some salespeople will. Some people win the lottery, too.)

Here's why:

1. Experienced salespeople are terrible at prospecting.

2. Experienced salespeople hate to prospect.

3. Even if a salesperson does do some prospecting successfully, as soon as they generate some pipeline, they become too busy to prospect. It's not sustainable.

Unless all I'm selling is big deals (>$250k), or I'm in an industry that truly is relationship-based (like the ad agency world), there is no way in hell I'm rolling the dice on my company based on the old-school idea, "hire some experienced salespeople, sick 'em on territories and let them sink or swim."

How Boards and CEOs Exacerbate The Problem

As soon as a product is ready for market and there is some initial customer traction, the board and CEO tend to rush to set 100%+ growth targets. They arbitrarily pick goals (since there's no data to base predictions on!) and turn the screws on the VP Sales. The VP Sales sucks it up (especially when he had no voice in the goals) and gets busy hiring salespeople... who miss plan. Company misses targets. Executive team is refreshed.

Why is it easier for people and companies to do more of what doesn't work than to take some time to figure out what does? By Q2, when the salespeople aren't making their 2010 numbers, there will be the push (from the board, CEO or VP Sales themselves) to hire more! "We're behind on our goals; we need to hire more salespeople!" How does that make sense?!

Why do CEOs and boards keep making this same dumb mistake? People, when under pressure or stress, tend to retreat to the safe place of what they know rather than taking the risk of trying new things. People tend to do more of what is not working rather than stepping back, taking a breather, and trying to figure out a new approach.

Some Answers

Unfortunately, there aren't any quick, repeatable fixes to this lead generation problem today. In fact, if you don't have any repeatable lead generation programs yet, you're already behind in getting ready for your goals in the coming 6-12 months.

Despite your investors' demands, it can take 2-12+ months to get lead generation cranking and generating predictable revenue. The time-to-results adds up fast: 1) there is the time spent on whether to start a new program and what it is, then 2) implementing it and (hopefully!) generating leads, and finally 3) adding in your sales cycle length of time... just to get your first incremental deal closed.

What works to generate flows of new leads:

- Trial-and-error in lead generation (requires patience, experimentation, money).
- "Marketing through teaching" via regular webinars, white papers, email newsletters and live events, to establish yourself

as the trusted expert in your space (takes lots of time to build predictable momentum).

- Patience in building great word-of-mouth (the highest value lead generation source, but hardest to influence).

- Cold Calling 2.0: By far the most predictable and controllable source of creating new pipeline, but it takes focus and expertise to do it well. Luckily, you are holding the guide to the process in your hands right now.

- Building an excited partner ecosystem (very high value, very long time-to-results).

- PR: It's great when, once in awhile, it generates actual results!

The time-to-results adds up fast. There is the time spent on whether to start a new program and what it is, then implementing it, generating leads (hopefully!), then adding in your sales cycle length of time...just to get your very first revenue deal closed.

Start With More Awareness

Start with more awareness on how much pipeline you're generating:

- Do your executive team and board know how much new (qualified) pipeline the company needs to generate per month? (This is the #2 most important metric to track, right after closed business.)

- Is the "new pipeline generated per month" number tracked at the board level?

- Is there a common language, common definitions, for "prospects," "leads" and "opportunities"? One of the biggest problems is usually mis-communication and misunderstanding of terms and metrics between executives and directors.

At least if your executive team and board are aware of the pipeline gap – the amount of pipeline required to hit your results, and likely places it will come from – you can begin to be more realistic in both your goals and plans to execute on those goals. You will also be less likely to break trust with your team and investors by missing your goals as a surprise, i.e., without really knowing why.

Have You Ever Felt Like An Utter Failure?

Every lesson in this book has been learned the hard way. (Yes, I used to be one of those CEOs making the fatal planning mistake in the prior section.)

What frustrations, challenges or failures are you facing right now, in life or work? Do you understand that from these challenges can come your biggest successes?

You've read on the cover of this book or on my blog that my sales process helped create $100 million in recurring revenue for Salesforce.com. The seed for that success (and the whole idea of "Predictable Revenue") was planted in an incredibly painful failure of my own.

Back in 1999, I was the founder and CEO of LeaseExchange.com, a 50-person Internet company. I learned the hard way what works and doesn't work in management and sales (basically by screwing up a lot and not asking for enough help from others). After raising $5 million in venture capital and working through it for a couple of years, we shut down the business in 2001.

The dream died.

Have you ever had a dream die? (I've been divorced too, which was even more painful. But don't hold your breath for a book on Predictable Love!) Have you ever been so excited about something in your life — more excited than about anything else, ever — only to have it crash and burn? It was ugly. And as a founder and leader, I felt responsible for killing the dreams of my people at the company.

During the "death march" while the company died, I spent too much time alone outside of work. I became a hermit--exactly the wrong thing to do when I needed community the most.

My escape during the closing of the company was drinking vodka while playing computer games on Friday nights, just to numb out and distract myself from what was going on.

And yes, once the doors on the company finally closed, I at least felt a little relief because the death march was over.

Looking back, I can be grateful for all the mistakes I made as a CEO and founder. Frankly, I was a *terrible* manager. As painful as it was, the experience of those years with LeaseExchange prepared me for success at Salesforce.com and with my current business, PebbleStorm.

When I joined Salesforce.com, I checked my ego at the door and took the most junior sales role there, which paid a total of $50,000 per year (and with very little stock, like .0002%).

I would like to say I almost didn't go to Salesforce.com, but I was determined to join them no matter what.

I went from being CEO of my own company, to answering the 1-800- sales line at Salesforce.com. (Has pride ever stopped you from doing something important for your happiness or future?)

In fact, if you registered on Salesforce.com's website in late 2002, it's likely I was the person that called and emailed you to find out if you were a possible lead.

I took the job because I strongly believed that before starting another company, I needed an MBA in building world-class sales organizations. I didn't want to learn how to create random revenue; I wanted to create predictable revenue.

And now, I know it's even MORE important than I thought, which is why I ended up writing this book. So many CEOs and Sales VPs make mistakes in building sales teams, wasting millions of dollars and years of time.

I ended up creating an entirely new sales process and inside sales team that helped Salesforce.com add $100 million in incremental recurring revenue over just a few short years. The team and process were sustainable, and is still going strong all these years later.

It was my failures that helped me see why it was worth it to me to start at the very bottom again. Now I can be grateful for my failures.

What are your biggest or most recent failures? What about them can you be grateful for? Can you anticipate how you will benefit by getting through your current challenges?

"Failure" is just your judgment on an experience, because there are no failures, just learning opportunities.

The $100 Million Sales Process

In 2003, Salesforce.com had a problem: it had hired a bunch of high-priced field salespeople to bring in and close new business, but they were starving for pipeline and leads. Their Rolodexes turned out to be, with very few exceptions, unhelpful. We had lots of expensive salespeople with thin pipelines.

Although Salesforce.com's marketing and PR machines were generating lots of leads, the leads were mostly from small businesses, not enterprises.

Except for knocking on doors when I had a painting business in college, I'd never done sales or lead generation before joining Salesforce.com.

Knowing nothing about lead generation and sales ended up helping me because I brought a fresh perspective to selling. After trying a few cold calls, I realized what a waste of time that kind of work was and immediately gave it up. Not only did I HATE cold calling (mostly because the people I called hated it), it was just totally ineffective. I knew there had to be a better way, something more enjoyable, interesting and productive.

I also read a bunch of sales books about selling and prospecting, and then threw them away. Most said the same things, in different ways, and weren't helpful at all. (Though they would have been great if we were in the 1980's.)

At first I felt really frustrated, because I felt like I had to start from scratch.

I ended up creating a sales prospecting process and inside sales team that consistently generated new qualified sales opportunities for the quota-carrying salespeople. Nearly everything changed.

The team no longer had to qualify website leads.

The team didn't handle sales order paperwork.

The team didn't close small deals.

The team didn't help out marketing.

The team wasn't distracted.

Instead, the team had a **single mission**: to generate (but not by cold calling; see Chapter 2) new qualified sales opportunities from cold companies (ones at which we had no activity or interest) and passing these qualified opportunities to quota-carrying salespeople to close.

The team only contacted cold new business accounts at which we didn't have a relationship or current interest, and past accounts which had gone cold for at least six months. The team didn't receive any new inbound leads generated by word-of-mouth or by marketing (these leads went specifically to a separate Market Response team to qualify and pass to Account Executives).

This sales lead generation process involved no cold calling, which I regarded as a waste of time after experimenting with making cold calls myself.

In addition to hiring great people and creating a proven, repeatable process, there were two other very important keys to the team's track record of year-after-year-after year of success:

1. **Predictable Results/ROI:** We had a simple sales prospecting process that was highly effective, repeatable, and very predictable. Our process and training system made it easy for sales reps to succeed, and 95% of them beat their numbers while ramping up.

   After about 12 months of results and data, we could predict the future results of new hires on my team. For example, I knew that if we hired someone costing $100,000 per year (including all their overhead), that person would generate per year as much as $3,000,000 in total contracts. I could also predict how long it would take for that person to ramp up and become cash flow positive to the company.

2. **Self-Managing Systems:** Everything was a system. I didn't want myself or any single person to be a bottleneck to the success of the team. What if I was hit by a bus? The team had to be self-managing so that it could grow and succeed.

Your sales results are only as scalable to the extent the CEO and executives are designed out of the process. Too many companies are dependent on the CEO or VP Sales for selling. How can you make the sales team and results independdent of their direct help, except for coaching?

Make Your Lack Of Money An Advantage

I definitely want you to use the techniques in this book to make more money more predictably. But don't just follow the process blindly, be creative. You need to control your own destiny and not let "reasons" get in the way of results.

What's holding you back from generating more leads and more predictable revenue? Do you think it's the market conditions or economy, a lack of money, not having the right people, technology hurdles?

One excuse I hear all the time is, "We don't have the marketing budget"; or, "We don't have the sales budget"; even "If we just had more money…." You don't need a lot of money to create the results and company (or even the life) you want. Lack of money is a common excuse for not being creative.

You, your CEO, your managers or employees can make all kinds of valid-sounding excuses about why a new idea, business or project isn't moving forward: you need more time, or more marketing money, or your people aren't motivated, or you need funding, etc.

There is ALWAYS a way to move forward, even without money.

None of these are real obstacles to moving forward to get what you want, whether it's more growth, predictable sales revenue, starting your own company, or turning your employees into mini-CEOs. There is ALWAYS a way to move forward, even without money.

Back to money and marketing budgets: Money can help, but you don't need a lot of marketing money in order to ramp up sales.

At Salesforce.com we spent zero dollars in marketing to create the outbound sales team and produce $100 million in results. The initial investment? One person's salary.

In case you're thinking, "Easy for you to say. Results came easy for you. You were a part of Salesforce.com. Your company was famous. You didn't need budget, you had branding. You had all kinds of support. What if I want to increase sales but don't have a big brand or big budget?"

True, Salesforce.com was always very well-known in the Bay Area and in the startup world. But when we began building the outbound sales team and targeting the "Fortune 5000" in 2003, very few large companies outside of California had heard of Salesforce.com. Nine out of ten times when we called a prospect, they asked something along the lines of, "Do you do outsourced sales for customers? Or do sales recruiting?"

Shelly Davenport, my manager at the time, and I had an interesting design challenge: to create an outbound sales process that would succeed without any money or marketing support and at a company that was pretty much unknown in the Fortune 2000 market we were growing into at the time.

This was also just after the dot-com bust, and trust of anything ".com" was at an all-time low.

Also, software-as-a-service was NOT yet accepted by large companies as a viable option. Gartner, a famous technology research firm, was still writing big reports about how Salesforce.com was a great fit for small businesses but not for larger companies.

While Salesforce.com spent millions on general marketing, most of it only reached small business decision makers.

In starting our outbound sales team, we didn't get a budget for my project beyond my own compensation. In fact, looking back, if I had had a big budget or a bunch of people to tell what to do, I wouldn't have been forced to get so creative in solving the problem of how to predictably generate new pipeline for the sales organization.

What We Did Have:

1. **A wholly committed person** (me) who could dedicate their full attention to the challenge (rather than giving it only 25% of my time);

2. **Two core tools:** the Salesforce.com application and an online source for lists of companies and contacts called OneSource (similar to Hoovers);

3. **Freedom** to experiment for three months as an internal entrepreneur or "mini-CEO";

4. An **optimistic attitude** that saw this as an interesting challenge, and it could be fun solving it;

5. A **commitment** to create something meaningful (in terms of sales) to Salesforce.com.

The point here is that when you're low on resources, by having a clear objective and looking at it as an interesting challenge, you can force yourself (and your employees) to GET CREATIVE.

Constraints often lead to more creativity from both yourself and your people. Don't let so-called "reality" stop you!

2

Cold Calling 2.0 – Ramp Sales Fast Without Cold Calls

Cold calling sucks! Isn't there a better way? Yep, and here it is.

The First Breakthroughs

I've gone back and forth a lot about the term "Cold Calling 2.0," mostly because it doesn't involve any cold calling. In fact, if you're making cold calls, you are doing everything wrong.

Cold Calling 2.0 means prospecting into cold accounts to generate new business without using any "cold calls." I define a cold call as "calling someone who doesn't know you and who isn't expecting your call." No one enjoys this – neither the caller nor the person being called, right?

Cold Calling 2.0 also means you have processes and a system in place to generate new pipeline and leads predictably – that is, an organization knows how "x effort" will lead to "y results". In fact, it can be the most predictable source of pipeline at a company, done right – as with companies like Salesforce.com, WPromote or Responsys.

While Cold Calling 2.0 is a system with many steps, there was one original breakthrough that started the snowball rolling.

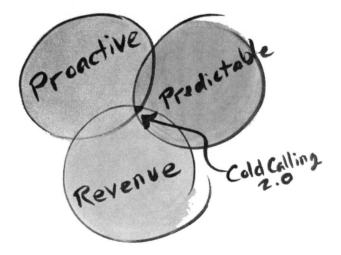

In early 2003 I was experimenting with regular cold calling, banging the phones, to see if it worked. Cold calling worked a little bit, and far too slowly: through cold calling, I found I could generate two highly qualified opportunities per month. I'm emphasizing high quality because frequently outbound sales teams pump up their results by throwing over lots of poorly-qualified demos and appointments to their Account Executives. So when I say "high quality," I mean it.

Back to March 2003...my goal was to generate at least eight highly qualified opportunities per month. I was doing two per month through cold calling. OUCH. How was I going to quadruple my results?

Breakthrough #1:

The biggest bottleneck in prospecting into companies that have more than a few executives isn't getting to the decision maker/influencer/point person...it's finding them in the first place!

Oftentimes the ultimate decision maker – such as the CEO or VP Sales in the case of Salesforce.com, is not the best person for your first conversations. And in larger companies, there can be so many people with the word "sales" or "marketing" in their title, it's impossible from the outside to tell who does what.

I learned this through hard work – cold calling, cold emailing, plugging away. I realized I spent most of my time hunting for the right person – not trying to sell or qualify them.

If I could find the right person, I could usually have a productive business conversation with them. But it took a LOT of time to find them, especially in those byzantine Fortune 5000 companies!

In Desperation, I Tried An Experiment

I'd always assumed that mass emailing executives wouldn't work. Don't I need to carefully craft each email to them to make it personal?

I wrote one email that was a classic cold calling letter: "Do you have these challenges? X, Y Z...."

I also wrote a totally "short and sweet" different email – in plain text, with no HTML -- simply asking for a referral to the right person at the company. (I don't share the actual email templates in this book for two reasons, which I will share in the section about email).

Here was a lesson learned in the value of a) not assuming anything, and b) experimenting:

19

On a Friday afternoon, I sent two mass emails from Salesforce.com:

100 of the "classic sales" emails to Fortune 5000 executives, and

100 of the "short and sweet" emails to the same kind of list.

Out of 200 emails I sent, the next morning when I checked email, I had 10 responses sitting in my inbox! Again, these were from C-level and VP-level executives at large companies – just the people with whom I wanted to talk.

Response rate for the "sales-y" email: 0%.

Response rate for the "short and sweet" email: 10%! (10 responses out of the 100 short and sweet emails.)

And at least five of the emails I received from the short and sweet campaign were positive, referring me to other people in the organization as the best person for a conversation about sales force automation.

Breakthrough #2:

Mass emailing C-level Fortune 5000 executives, with specific kinds of emails, can generate 9%+ response rates.

Those high response rates (7-9% or more) from high-level executives have held true year after year, even with my current clients in 2011, seven years later.

A 500% Increase In Results

In the next month, April 2003, I increased my results by 500% and generated 11 highly qualified sales opportunities that continued on in live sales cycles. (And this increase in opportunities did later lead to an equal increase in revenue.)

The tipping point of the Cold Calling 2.0 process was born: sending mass emails to high level executives to ask for referrals to the best person in their organization for a first conversation.

The Complexities Of High-Volume And Growth

It's one thing for a single person to send out emails and generate responses in a week or a month. It's another to create a regular stream of opportunities that come in from that person and a whole team year after year.

Your first email campaign is just a first step of a much longer journey.

Much of the Cold Calling 2.0 content in this book (and outside of this book) relates to ensuring your system predictably generates results over years, and with almost any kind of salesperson or size of team.

Terms And Abbreviations

Everyone uses all kinds of different terms in sales. Here are the main terms I use in this book, and what they mean:

- **Sales Development Representative (or "SDR")**: This is a Cold Calling 2.0 or "outbound" sales rep. Ideally they are specialized, just generating outbound leads. They neither close deals nor qualify inbound website leads.

- **Outbound Sales Rep:** Another term for an "SDR."

- **Account Executive (or "AE")**: A quota-carrying salesperson, whether they are an inside sales rep or in the field.

- **Market Response Rep (or "MRR")**: An inside salesperson who only qualifies leads coming in from a website.

- **Sales Force Automation (or "SFA")**: Software or internet-based services that sales teams use to manage all of their contacts and accounts, automate sales processes, and report on sales results.

- **Customer Relationship Management (or "CRM")**: Software- or internet-based services that typically include Sales Force Automation functions plus features for marketing and customer service, so that all of the main ways a company interacts with customers is managed through a single system.

Within a company, misunderstanding of terms and roles is a common source of confusion in executive teams. Ensure your people have a set of terms that are agreed upon and everybody understands.

RIP Cold Calling

Why Aren't Old Techniques Effective Anymore?

Although once in awhile a cold call or classic new business letter might work, it's becoming rarer. There are three dynamics in the market that have changed the nature of prospecting and what works:

1. **Buyers are sick of being sold to**, and become more resistant every year to classic sales and marketing methods, such as pushy cold calls or generic marketing materials.

2. **Sales 2.0 technologies**, both of CRM systems and Sales 2.0 applications, make it easier than ever to take the guesswork out of implementing, executing and auditing the ROI of a prospecting methodology.

3. **More accountability on marketing budgets.** There is ever-increasing pressure for lead generation and marketing budgets to show documented proof of revenue results. Every project is scrutinized: "What's the ROI? How do you know?" Executives want proof of revenue generated. Have you ever done a careful measurement of your cold calling programs? Chances are they are much more productive in terms of amount of activity than revenue. Executives are taking closer looks at these programs, and not liking what they see.

How Is Cold Calling 2.0 Different?

I define a cold call is "calling someone who doesn't know you and who isn't expecting your call."

Cold Calling 2.0 means prospecting into cold accounts without ever making any cold calls. More importantly though, executed systematically in high-volume, an inside Sales Development team devoted exclusively to Cold Calling 2.0 can become the most predictable and sustainable pipeline engine (and thus revenue) for the company.

Three key principles to developing a team successfully include:

1. **No cold calling!** Prospect into cold accounts with new methods, other than surprising people on the phone or trying to negotiate around gatekeepers. For example, use simple emails to generate referrals to the right people, who then expect (and often welcome) your call.

2. **A focus on results, not activities!** That means that dials and calls per day, or even appointments set, are much less interesting or even important. Rather, track metrics such as qualification calls per day or week, and qualified opportunities per month. Calls per day and dials are usually only tracked during training periods, for coaching purposes while reps ramp up their pipelines.

3. **Everything is systematically process-driven!** This includes management practices, hiring, training, and of course, the actual prospecting process. By emphasizing repeatability and consistency, the pipeline and revenue ramps generated by a new Sales Development Rep become very predictable, and the entire team's results become highly sustainable.

You must carve out time to work on these "important but not urgent" priorities. As with eating well and staying away from junk food, it takes discipline and commitment to follow these principles. If you fall into the trap of being "so busy you can't get anything done," you will have incredible challenges in building a foundation of success for your future.

Salesforce.com's Cold Calling 2.0 Story

In 2002, Saleforce.com had begun building a field sales organization dedicated to larger companies. To supplement the inbound leads they received (generated mostly through word-of-mouth), the field sales force was expected to prospect to bring in their own large deals. However, little was happening in the way of prospecting.

Salesforce.com realized that in addition to the field people not making many calls because of their understandable dislike for cold calls, the ones who were trying to generate their own business were simply ineffective at it.

The environment had changed, and the traditional prospecting techniques of the 1990's weren't working. Not only were cold calls ineffective, but also targeted marketing programs offering high value items (such as business books) produced disappointing results.

Making the field salespeople do cold calls means having your highest-cost (per hour) sales resource perform the lowest-value (per hour) activity.

Salesforce.com decided it needed a new approach to create its own controllable, predictable source of new pipeline.

We began the Cold Calling 2.0 project in early 2003, and spent a year testing and perfecting the methodology and system to prove its ability to add incremental revenue at a high ROI, before heavily investing in building a team around it.

Why We Refined And Tested The Process For A Year

While it took me four months to generate my first highly successful month of new opportunities and qualified pipeline, management had two valid concerns to address before they invested heavily:

Will the pipeline turn into revenue? In other words: Will the deals close?

Can junior salespeople do this too, that is, can it scale?

We promoted a junior salesperson to be a second member on my team. I trained him and he quickly began generating the same results as I had. Also, over the second half of 2003, a significant amount of pipeline closed.

25

We ended the year with more than $1,000,000 in new bookings (at least $3,000,000 in lifetime value), which cost less than $150,000 to generate (about 1.5 fully-loaded salaries).

No wonder that in early 2004 the Salesforce.com management team decided to grow the Cold Calling 2.0 effort from two people to twelve!

A key advantage we had was the Salesforce.com application itself. We would never have produced the same level of results without using Salesforce.com's software. The traditional sales systems (such as ACT, Goldmine, Siebel) would have held us back as slow, unintuitive and lacking the capabilities we needed around things like easy sharing of a common database, reporting and dashboards. They could have worked for a small team of one or two people, but they wouldn't have been able to keep up with our team's growth as we grew to six, twelve, twenty, etc.

Despite some serious obstacles, which are detailed below, results quickly followed!

Revenue

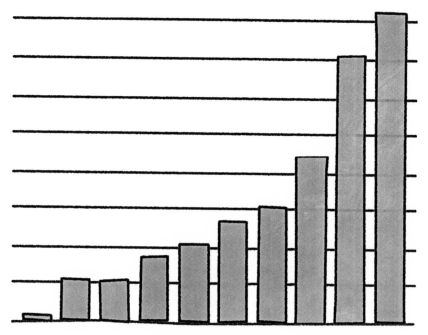

Serious Cold Calling 2.0 Challenges At Salesforce.com

You might assume that the prospecting was easy "just because it was Salesforce.com," now a well known brand, and those companies would take our calls. Nothing could be further from the truth. Although today Salesforce.com is a globally recognized brand company and the Software-as-a-Service (SaaS) licensing model is broadly accepted, back in the early and mid-2000's, things were different:

Salesforce.com was unknown and misunderstood in most companies. If someone had heard of Salesforce.com, they typically thought, "Don't you offer outsourced sales teams?"

Salesforce.com was pioneering the concept of Software-as-a-Service, offering its products online and on-demand; SaaS had not yet become accepted by mainstream companies.

Furthermore, traditional prospecting techniques just didn't work. (That's why I decided to throw out all the books and legacy ideas and start from scratch. Because I had zero sales experience prior to Salesforce.com, I had a fresh perspective.)

All of these factors stood in our way – but we didn't give up. The executive team gave me the time (four months) I needed to keep experimenting until I could create a process that worked.

Are you making excuses (which may sound like extremely logical reasons) for not finding ways to get around your challenges?

Cold Calling 1.0 Vs. Cold Calling 2.0

Here are examples of the different intentions and practices of Cold Calling 1.0 versus Cold Calling 2.0, following many of the trends that have affected all kinds of selling:

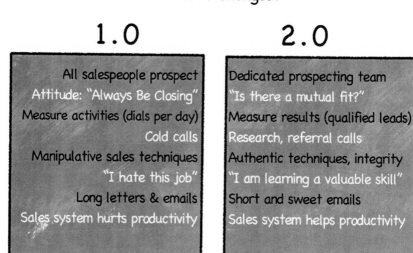

What's Changed?

1.0	2.0
All salespeople prospect	Dedicated prospecting team
Attitude: "Always Be Closing"	"Is there a mutual fit?"
Measure activities (dials per day)	Measure results (qualified leads)
Cold calls	Research, referral calls
Manipulative sales techniques	Authentic techniques, integrity
"I hate this job"	"I am learning a valuable skill"
Long letters & emails	Short and sweet emails
Sales system hurts productivity	Sales system helps productivity

Here are some further thoughts on what has changed:

1. Develop respected experts: The Sales Development role is often treated within a sales organization as a low-level job. If you treat it that way, you'll get low-level results. It's a challenging and often thankless role. Treat the team as, and expect them to be, experts. Don't skimp on training, equipping or developing them. Set high expectations of their ongoing skills development.

2. Qualify accounts and contacts before calling: Cold Calling 1.0 involves calling or emailing into unfiltered industry-based lists of targets. Prospecting into accounts of marginal potential is the most common waste of time by Sales Development Reps and companies. Spend serious time on identifying and clarifying your Ideal Customer Profile. Define what companies are the most similar to your top 5-10% of your customers, defined as the ones likeliest to purchase for the most revenue, and develop focused target lists based on these tight criteria.

3. Research rather than sell: When reps do call into cold accounts, rather than cold calls, make "research calls." The intention is different – rather than trying to get the decision maker on the phone, a rep simply learns about the company and whether there is even a potential fit or not.

4. Blackberry-sized emails: Avoid sending long sales emails that no one reads. Send emails that are very short (readable on a blackberry) and to the point. Be honest and to the point – what are you looking for?

5. Go beyond basic SFA: Leverage your sales force automation ("SFA") systems in every way possible. For example, you MUST use dashboards. What about applications for de-duplication and data cleansing, contact acquisition, or tools that tell you when prospects that you are in touch with visit your website? There is a wealth of options now to enhance every step of your process – in fact, there are so many options it can be confusing! Don't let that stop you from constantly testing new applications to see what works for your company.

Could Cold Calling 2.0 Work For My Company?

Are people involved in the process of finding new clients?

Are your customers worth more than $5,000 to you? (It can work for smaller amounts, but it will be harder for you to make it profitable).

Then this can work for you, whether you're selling products or services.

The results we created aren't unique to Salesforce.com. For example, Responsys was the very first company Erythean Martin, my partner at the time, and I worked with to help implement the system.

Within four months they increased the pipeline generated per Sales Development person by 300% and Cold Calling 2.0 become the top (and most predictable) source of new pipeline for in the company.

The Cold Calling 2.0 process works for consulting and services companies as well, though it is more challenging. Professional services companies tend to have developed their business based more on relationships and brand than on specific benefits. Services companies have to spend extra time honing in on their Ideal Customer Profiles and their challenges, to make this worthwhile. Of course, this is necessary for any lead generation project, not just Cold Calling 2.0.

Ultimately, if the will and commitment exists in the CEO and executive team to make it happen, and they can let go of their past cold calling assumptions and follow this new process, it will work.

Why Account Executives Should Not Make Cold Calls

There are three problems with expecting your Account Executives (quota carrying salespeople) -- whether they are inside or field based -- to be the ones to do all the work developing new accounts:

- They don't like to do it.
- They usually aren't any good at it (or are even terrible at it).
- It's a poor use of company resources by using the most expensive sales role to do lower-value work.

Where And When Account Executives Should Prospect

Here are the rules of thumb about where Account Executives should spend their precious time prospecting:

- A short, targeted "Top 5" or "Top 10" list of strategic accounts to penetrate.
- Their current customer base.
- Developing referral or channel partners.

The point is to focus your highest value people on the low-volume but high-value activities (building relationships at key accounts), and specialize other roles and sales reps to take over low-value yet high-volume activities (prospecting into untargeted cold accounts).

Case Study

Cold Calling 2.0 Example: HyperQuality Triples Results In 90 Days

Note from Aaron: My partner Marylou Tyler was a natural with the Cold Calling 2.0 outbound sales process! Here's how she helped her first Cold Calling 2.0 client triple their results in 90 days.

A Problem Of Inbound Inquiries

HyperQuality, Inc., a Seattle-based contact center quality assurance solution provider, has been around for seven years, with customers such as Barclays, Sirius FM, Carlson Travel, AT&T, Orkin, Vonage, and Travelocity. Customers subscribe to their service for $100,000 to $1+ million per year, so every high-quality lead matters, and they used to be hard to generate.

Until they met Marylou, HyperQuality got most of their leads from inbound inquiries from people who e-mailed, filled out forms on their website, or called their 800 number. While the flow of inbound inquiries was consistent, thanks largely to the efforts they made in their search engine optimization ("SEO") and pay-per-click ("PPC") programs, too many of the inquiries were low quality leads that didn't fit HyperQuality's qualification criteria. Some common reasons included:

- **Budget:** There was no defined budget or the budget was far too small.

- **Authority:** The decision maker had no idea that someone lower-level in their organization was doing research, and had no intention of becoming involved.

- **Need:** The inbound lead didn't have a recognized problem, they were just "looking around".

- **Timing:** The inquiry had no timeframe, or the timing was too far in the future to be serious.

- **Fit:** The inquiry needed a service or product that HyperQuality's didn't provide.

HyperQuality generated 1-2 inbound leads per month that passed their rigorous qualification standards. To meet their growth targets, they needed a drastic increase in pipeline. Also, the quota-carrying Account Executives also qualified leads coming in from the website, which meant they spend a lot of expensive time following up on inquiries that went nowhere.

Stop Doing More Of What Doesn't Work

Bob Kelly, Senior Vice President of Sales & Marketing at HyperQuality, knew he needed a better way to fill the pipeline for his sales team. He brought in Marylou Tyler to implement the Cold Calling 2.0 outbound sales process.

Under Bob's leadership and commitment to the change, his sales teams completely embraced this "new" way of prospecting, including:

- Creating a new, dedicated outbound sales development role focused 100% on outbound prospecting.
- Never making another cold call again, and instead using the Cold Calling 2.0 email process to easily get referrals to decision makers at accounts.
- The closers focused on their live pipeline, closing deals and only prospected to a small number of strategic accounts.

Companies *must* make these kinds of changes in order to create a highly effective outbound sales team.

Testing & Refining

Bob and the team met weekly with Marylou to review the progress of the new initiative. Each week, the first topic discussed on the company-wide sales agenda was the new outbound sales process, reviewing metrics such as:

- Email response rates (usually 7-10%)
- What e-mails are companies responding to, and why
- Who is responding (title, position of authority)
- Number of Scoping Calls completed
- Who became a qualified opportunity, and why
- Refinements to the Ideal Customer Profile (which was revised many, many times)

With this consistent focus on making the new process work (and following the step-by-step process to the letter), the team began to get responses from targeted accounts in days and a flow of high-level appointments in weeks.

The Pipeline Tripled Like "Magic"

Within 90 days, HyperQuality went from generating two leads to eight per month that fit HyperQuality's strict criteria...and this was just with part-time prospecting work by one person. *(Aaron note: once ramped up, a single full-time outbound rep can generate 10-20 excellent leads per month.)*

The process and Marylou's help was called "magic" by the sales team!

Just like Salesforce.com and HyperQuality, companies that implement the Cold Calling 2.0 process can turn pipeline generation off-and-on like a faucet, by changing the number of dedicated outbound prospectors on the team and how much outreach they do, and create an ability to penetrate new industries or geographic markets at will (the process also works in Asia and Europe).

3

Executing Cold Calling 2.0

OK — so how do you do it? This isn't a true step-by-step manual (which would go beyond the scope of this book), but it will give you enough direction to get going on your own.

Getting Started With Cold Calling 2.0

The following sections contain a lot of specific details and steps on how you can get started on your own with this process. Much more detailed how-to's and training videos can be obtained through our products and coaching.

To begin implementing the Cold Calling 2.0 system, you should have:

- At least one person 100% dedicated to prospecting (or you intend to have this person). Yes, you can start part-time, but it will be hard to get significant results until you have someone totally committed to it.

- You have some kind of sales system that lets your sales team share and manage their sales contacts and accounts. Salesforce.com is still the best system (in my humble though admittedly biased opinion) but what's more important is that you have something beyond spreadsheets, whiteboards and email.

- Your prospects use email.

- You have a proven product or service that has generated revenue.

- The "lifetime value of a customer" is more than $10,000 (the more the better). The process will definitely work if your lifetime value is lower (especially if you're a single-owner business doing this for yourself), but it becomes more challenging to make it profitable through hired salespeople.

Experiment To Make It Work For You

Every business is different, and things work differently for each salesperson. The idea here is to give you a set of tools, with some guidance, that you can experiment with and customize to make work for your own special situation.

Remember: *Treat these tools with an attitude of experimentation.* Play with them. Find out what works best for you.

The Most Important First Step

If you want to take an important step towards turning your sales organization into a sales machine, start by letting your Account Executives (the sales reps closing business) focus on what they do best: work active sales cycles and close.

Let a different role, Sales Development Reps, focus on generating new qualified opportunities for your Account Executives.

As a first step, dedicate a role (whether you begin with one person or a whole team) to ONLY doing outbound prospecting activities. Break it off from inbound lead qualification and from closing.

This is so important that I mention it several times in this book: **Specialize, Specialize, Specialize!**

Implement a Sales Development function to prospect for new clients to ensure a predictable, sustainable supply of qualified leads for the field and/or telesales teams, and a Market Response function to qualify the leads that come into your website, through the telephone or other "inbound" channels.

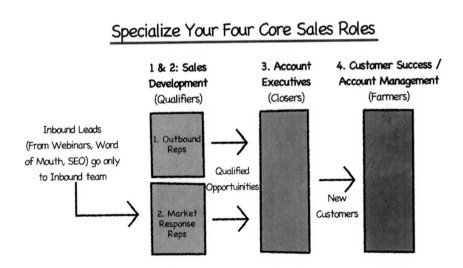

Specialize Your Four Core Sales Roles

1. Sales Development Reps prospect into cold or inactive companies who aren't engaging with you already, to source new, incremental sales opportunities and pass them to quota-carrying salespeople.

In the past this team would have been making cold calls, though today there are much more effective ways to prospect. Organize Sales Development Reps by territories that match the field and telesales reps, because it's vital for them to build relationships with their sales teammates.

One Sales Development Rep typically can support a maximum of 2-5 quota-carrying Account Executives. If you sell very large deals, it's possible you could have even a 1-to-1 ratio or 2-to-1 Sales Development Reps per Account Executive and still be VERY profitable.

By the way, while adding a dedicated Sales Development function can vastly improve your outbound prospecting results, we're not saying your quota-carrying salespeople should not do any new business generation – far from it!

However, Account Executive closers shouldn't spend their time making cold calls. They should focus on higher-potential sources of business: a small list of targeted accounts at which they can build relationships, current clients, or their own past dead opportunities.

2. Market Response Reps qualify incoming leads that reach the company through the website or phone (usually driven either by internet search, word-of-mouth or marketing programs), and route qualified opportunities to the appropriate quota-carrying salesperson.

A rule of thumb is that for every 400 leads per month that require human attention, a company needs one Market Response Representative.

By removing unqualified opportunities out of the pipeline early in the sales cycle, Market Response determines which accounts will be followed up by the sales force and thereby paves the way for increased close rates by the field and telesales, who spend their time only on pre-qualified opportunities.

Why Sales Development and Market Response Should Be Separated

In companies where incoming lead volume justifies having a dedicated market response function, separate the Market Response from Sales Development to make both teams more focused and productive.

The roles are very different (inbound reps receive leads to work to qualify, while outbound reps initiate calls and emails), and it's very challenging for a rep to switch between the two mindsets throughout the day.

The Market Response Reps become experts at efficiently qualifying inbound and marketing-generated leads, and the Sales Development team only prospects for incremental business at accounts that need to be pursued, where there is no active or pre-existing interest.

How We Learned This The Hard Way At Salesforce.com

Salesforce.com learned this the hard way in 2004, when we changed from having separate Sales Development teams doing inbound and outbound roles, to having the same team handle both inbound and outbound responsibilities.

Within a week, productivity had dropped by 30%. Within three weeks, it was clear that the productivity drop was caused by the mixing of the responsibilities and was not going to improve with time. Salesforce.com quickly changed the structure back to separate teams doing Sales Development and Market Response functions, and productivity rose back to prior levels.

It was this kind of specialization that was important to helping achieve massive breakthroughs in results. Through 2008, the Cold Calling 2.0 team at Salesforce.com (the "Enterprise Business Representative Team") had sourced about $100 million in recurring annual revenue for Salesforce.com. Year after year, return on investment on each person in the role was about 3000%.

Choosing A Sales Force Automation System

Perhaps you've never known anything except Salesforce.com. Perhaps you've never heard of Salesforce.com!

Having worked at Salesforce.com for four years, and done consulting with dozens of companies since then, I've talked with customers of every kind of system you can imagine.

While it is far from perfect, Salesforce.com is still (as of 2011) the best sales force automation system out there. There are good reasons why more than a MILLION people use it, and why they do more than $1 BILLION in revenue per year.

My sales team could never have produced the results and level of productivity without Salesforce.com, which enabled us to do more and produce higher quality work.

Having said that, whichever system you choose and use, the most important thing is that you use it. If you're having problems benefiting from it, remember a system is just a tool – it's more likely that the problems are coming from the users, not the tool itself.

And CEOs, remember: people follow your example. The more you live in your system, the more your people will use it.

The Source Of Predictability: Cold Calling 2.0 Funnel

Here is the source your PREDICTABLE REVENUE comes from: predictable lead generation.

For companies selling high-value products or services, the most predictable source of leads (whether or not it's the largest source) can be outbound sales prospecting.

Here is a sample funnel that breaks out the prospecting stages:

Example Cold Calling 2.0 Funnel

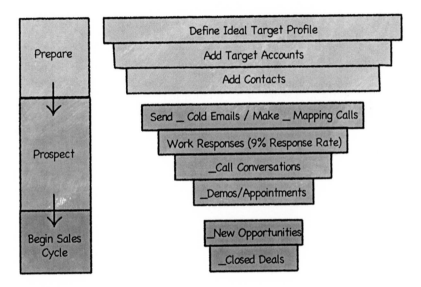

As you can see, if you experiment with your process, people and activities to find how to generate a predictable flow of new qualified opportunities, and have a consistent sales closing rate, you can begin to generate highly predictable revenue and proactive growth.

Revenue Predictability = The Funnel + Average Deal Size + Time

In addition to these activities and results funnel, you also have to know how long things take in order to have more predictability.

Time: Ramping New Reps

Measure and pay attention to the reality (rather than your unrealistic expectations) of how long your reps take to ramp up their results.

This amount of time can and will vary widely from company to company, depending on your lead flow, the people you hire, how well you train them, and whether they're picking up an established territory or starting a brand new one.

My advice: Put new reps through some kind of training program that has them working in other parts of your company first, talking to customers, before they go on active sale duty. This will make them much more effective salespeople and actually ramp them faster. Slow down to speed up!

Time: Prospecting and Sales Cycle Lengths

How long does it take for a prospector to generate a qualified opportunity? How long does it take for those opportunities to close? Are small ones faster than large ones? What are some imperfect but useful rules of thumb for you?

Prospecting cycle length: Measure the time between a) when the prospect first responds to a campaign to b) when a quality opportunity is created or qualified (this means the quota-carrying Account Executive has re-qualified and accepted the opportunity that the prospector passed over).

Incidentally, my rule of thumb is that it takes 2-4 weeks, on average, to qualify a new opportunity from an initial response.

Sales cycle length: I like to measure the time from a) when the opportunity was created or qualified to b) when it closed.

If you have trouble measuring this, just sit down with your reps and have a 15 minute conversation to talk about the last 10 deals that closed, to get a rough ballpark of the length.

Example:

To use realistic numbers, let's assume:

- A new prospector takes two months to ramp to full quota.
- Each rep produces 10 new, qualified opportunities per month.
- Deal size is $100,000

In this case, after two months an outbound rep will be producing $1 million in new qualified pipeline per month.

Now, if:

- Sales win rates are 20%, and
- Sales cycles average six months...

...then each new prospecting rep (working with their quota-carrying Account Executives) will be adding an incremental $200,000 in new revenue each month, with the flow really beginning about eight months after the outbound rep was hired (or six months after they reached full production).

Does eight months seem like a long time in our world of quick-fixes? What if you had started this team or this process eight months ago, wouldn't you love having that revenue right now?

Once you get this machine rolling, like a flywheel, this predictable source of new leads will keep producing revenue.

How Cold Calling 2.0 Works – The Process

Here is an overview of the Cold Calling 2.0 process, for a Sales Development Rep that is doing it full-time and passing opportunities to a quota-carrying salesperson.

If you are a sales rep who can only prospect part-time, adjust the goals accordingly (send half of the volume of outbound emails, for example), and obviously the last step ("pass the baton") won't apply to you.

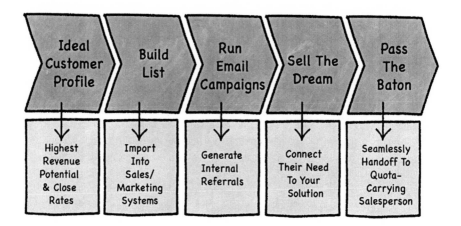

Step 1. Get Clear On Your Ideal Customer Profile

The simple most important thing you can do to make this program effective is to spend time getting clear on who your ideal customers are – both the kinds of accounts and the types of contacts in them.

This is where most companies fall short from the start, by targeting the wrong prospects, at the wrong levels, going after too many kinds of companies, or not speaking in 'their language'.

Step 2: Build Your List

How can you build a database of the above kinds of prospects? Do you already have a list in-house? Can you buy one? Or do you need to build one from scratch…?

Most companies approach and sell too low. Do you have decision-makers (or their bosses) as well as lower level people? How targeted is your list? Is it cluttered with non-relevant companies or people?

Resist any temptation to throw in lists of random prospects just because you have them – there is an opportunity cost to marketing to poor-fit prospects. Responses from people who don't fit your customer criteria will just end up wasting your time and cluttering your database.

Step 3. Run Outbound Email Campaigns

Don't make this mistake: companies are too dependent on cold calls. Phone skills are critical, but use calls as the second step in prospecting. Begin with email, and then use phone to follow up to people who respond. Simple email templates can get you an 8-12%-plus response rate even from high-level prospects.

Send outbound mass emails or mass voicemails to prospects that fit your Ideal Customer Profile. These emails should look as if they are a single email that came from a salesperson. They should be text-based, not fancy HTML (though you can use HTML templates that look like text).

Rather than sending hundreds of mass emails at a time in big bursts, the idea here is to send a regular, smaller number (50-100) of emails per salesperson each day, a few days a week, as a rolling campaign. The main goal of this stage is to generate just 5-10 new responses per day. Reps can't handle more responses than that per day without dropping balls.

Step 4. Sell The Dream

Do this: Work your responses and referrals to make contact with the right executives, and then "Sell The Dream." by helping them paint a vision of what kinds of solutions will solve their problems. Then connect your solution to their key business issue(s) and dream.

Don't treat your front-line sales reps as appointment-setting machines... setting up all kinds of meetings to which prospects don't show up. Do you have outbound reps that are only trained to push product, read from scripts or push demos? Or can they create a vision with a prospect and start building trust, credibility and rapport?

Step 5. Pass The Baton (With Dedicated Sales Development Reps)

If all your prospecting is done by your quota-carrying sales reps, you are making a fatal mistake. If you are committed to the results you want, you must have a team of reps dedicated to outbound prospecting, who generate new qualified opportunities to pass to closers to run with. There is a science to doing this, including transferring over the relationship, in ways that generate consistent and quality results.

It is vital that you have a simple and clear process to pass new leads smoothly from your dedicated prospectors to your quota-carrying Account Executives. Don't let anyone drop the baton!

First, I'll share a sample Cold Calling 2.0 Prospecting Funnel, and then in the following sections I'll go into each step in more detail.

Step 1: Get Clear On Your Ideal Customer Profile

What is the most important exercise you MUST do to get better results from marketing and sales? Answer: Get clear on your Ideal Customer Profile, including how to describe them, and what their core challenges are. You'll need to revise it many times before you feel "clear" – this is not a one-time exercise.

The Ideal Customer Profile (ICP) helps us maximize sales and marketing productivity by:

- Finding great prospects more easily through smart targeting; and,
- Disqualifying poor prospects more quickly.

(Both of which lead us to faster sales cycles and higher win rates.)

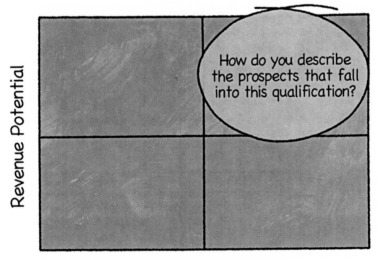

This is a collection of sample Ideal Customer Profile criteria purely for illustrative purposes, with both positive and red flags. You will need to rewrite all of them from scratch, including adding or subtracting different types of criteria. The ICP should, ideally, fit on a single page.

Design it this way to keep it simple: when we hire a new employee, how can you educate them as quickly as possible about what kinds of companies they should be striving to work with, or avoid?

Smart Targeting

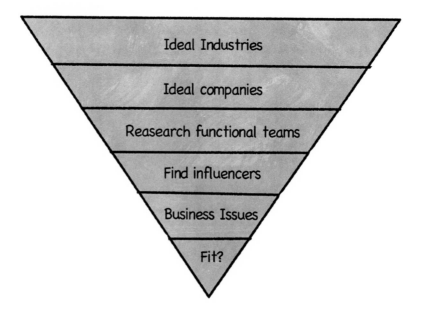

You don't need this many criteria as are listed below – even 3-5 key ones will help you. In fact, fewer, better criteria will make it easier to benefit from this exercise....

Criteria We Want	Why
25-250 Employees	Our customers have to be large enough to need our service. However, if they are too large, they tend to hire someone in-house to do it full-time.
Industries	The industries we are most successful in are media, technology, and business services.
Sales model	They have a direct sales organization, with at least 3 sales reps in place and a sales manager.
Spend more than $___ per month on ____	This function is important to them, and they can afford us.
Financial Status	Growing or profitable businesses have been our best long-term customers. Struggling companies usually end up as problematic customers.

No ad agency in place	If they have an ad agency they won't work with us, unless they are looking to replace their agency.
Values, people	The people we deal with are smart, honest, responsible, collaborative and respectful. Our best long-term customers have been the ones that we like as friends.
No in-house person	If there is a person in the company whose sole responsibility is _____, they see us as unnecessary.
Current System	They should have some kind of ___ system in place; optimally it would be ____ or ____.

Red Flags And Deal Breakers

What signals or signs can you look for, as early in the sales process as possible, to warn you (and the client) that working together is a waste of time? Here are some examples of red flags:

- They just installed a _____ kind of system.
- They already have an agency/service provider in place, or a full-time in-house person dedicated to ___.
- They churn-and-burn the consultants or agencies they hire to do _____.
- Know-it-alls / "We know what we're doing."
- Geography.
- Their monthly budget for _____ is only _____.
- These industries never seem to work: _____, _____, _____.
- This area of work is totally new to them, and they don't understand it yet. (That is, you would have to do a lot of education of the client before they would even understand the value of your service.)

Ideal Contacts

You should also apply this exercise to the kinds of buyers and influencers you work with, who buy from you.

"Our ideal contact is a VP Sales who is new to their role (less than 90 days in), who is looking to make things happen. They are process-oriented, report to the CEO or division president, and love data and reports. Their challenges include not being able to give accurate reports to their CEO because of problems with their sales system or the data in it..."

Their Core Challenges

As a final exercise in getting clear on your ideal customer profile, what are the core challenges of the company and of the individuals involved in the buying process?

You can learn these easily – just by asking! Whether by phone or by an online survey like SurveyMonkey, ask prospects and clients questions such as:

- What are your greatest challenges?
- What keeps you up at night?
- What are your main frustrations?
- What are you afraid of?
- What's most important to you?
- What do you spend money on?
- What do you really, really, REALLY want?

Refresh Regularly

Finally, you can have more than one kind of "ideal customer" and you also might have "ideal partners." Limit yourself to 1-5 types of profiles. If you think you need more than that, your marketing strategy needs focusing.

Step 2: Building Your List Of Targets

There are books and online resources about how to build marketing lists; that topic is beyond the scope of this book. This section will, however, point you in the right direction if you're unsure where to begin.

Different sources of leads and contacts are appropriate for different businesses. Targeting Fortune 5000? Try out OneSource. Targeting small business? Avoid OneSource and go for InfoUSA (as one example). Jigsaw (now owned by Salesforce.com) is perhaps the best general-purpose source of contacts with email addresses.

For individual sales reps or marketing directors selling to businesses larger than a couple hundred employees, we recommend using the popular services, most of which also integrate into Salesforce.com and perhaps other sales applications:

- Jigsaw (now owned by Salesforce.com)
- OneSource
- Hoovers
- InsideView
- ZoomInfo
- DataSalad (which is unique in that it has databases of companies that use certain applications, as I describe in the next section)

ZoomInfo vs. Jigsaw

At the time of this printing, my partner Marylou Tyler, the CEO of PredictableRevenue.com, had just completed a preliminary test of the quality of data between Jigsaw and ZoomInfo.

In short, she was surprisingly impressed that ZoomInfo had much higher quality of data, with 1) a much lower bounce rate and 2) higher response rate from prospects.

I'll leave the numbers out because it was a single first test, but check back on PredictableRevenue.com for a final conclusion.

What If We Are Selling To A Unique Market?

Do the above services not meet your needs?

It's amazing what kinds of lists and data overseas firms can build for you – although you will have to accept that the quality may not be great. Elance. com is an excellent resource to post projects and receive multiple bids from overseas vendors.

Blog Post On List Building

Brian Carroll has a nice post here to help you think about building lists: http://blog.startwithalead.com/weblog/2007/03/would_you_buy_t.html

DataSalad: Fresh B2B Marketing Data

When running the Salesforce.com lead generation team, I wish I would have had lists of the customers of competitors such as Oracle, Siebel and NetSuite.

In 2008 I founded DataSalad with Brian Mackley, because he had a technology that could produce those kinds of lists, and we were both tired of all the junky lists and data sources being hocked and resold. Another ex-Salesforce.com colleague, John Bogard, joined us as a partner in 2010.

DataSalad has lists of companies that are clients of and use specific applications — such as a list of customers of Salesforce.com, a list of Webex customers, and much more.

Where The Lists And Data Come From

People and companies leave all kinds of "digital fingerprints" on the Web. DataSalad generates the list of application-specific customers by crawling dozens of different sources of online information and databases, such as job boards and discussion groups.

Then the technology interprets these fingerprints and fragments to reassemble the data together into full records. The data is verified and cross-checked prior to being added to our database.

DataSalad maintains lists of application-specific customers of companies like Salesforce.com, NetSuite, Webex, Oracle, SAP, GreatPlains and more.

Just as with the other sources, you have to try some lists, A/B split-test and measure results to determine what works best for your company.

Step 3: Run Outbound Email Campaigns

The primary tool used by your outbound prospectors to get in front of new prospects is mass emailing. First, use email to generate internal referrals to the right person(s) at the target company. Then follow up on the responses and referrals with phone calls.

Ideally the reps are sending these mass emails through either your Sales Force Automation system (like Salesforce.com), or through a marketing automation system that integrates to your Sales Force Automation System. On any given day, the rep should send 50-100 targeted mass emails with a goal of having 5-10 responses per day (assuming about a 10% response rate).

"Targeted" mass emails sounds like an oxymoron. Here's how they're targeted: filter your list carefully according to the specific kind of account or contact you want to touch. Examples of filters include:

1. Vertical (retail, finance, high tech, etc)
2. Revenue
3. Geography / Territory
4. Employee count
5. Business model (B2B, B2C, agency)
6. Last Contact Activity Date
7. Last Account Activity Date
8. Contact Title (CEO, Director of Marketing, etc.)
9. Virtually anything else you are tracking

So even if you have a database of thousands of names, an SDR can segment down their total prospect pool into small groups that can be messaged with highly relevant information.

Writing Your Emails

Although I share my email templates with clients, I don't share email templates here for two reasons:

1. When you copy someone else's template, you lose your company's authentic voice.
2. If everyone uses the same email templates, the templates will likely lose their effectiveness.

Below are some guidelines for writing your own templates. If you don't want to reinvent the wheel, or are struggling to get your response rates up, we have products with templates you can purchase.

Guidelines For Writing Your Own Emails

These are guidelines for writing emails to cold prospects to start a conversation. Once you begin communicating, you can shift towards longer emails with more content, but in the beginning:

- These emails should look as if they are a single email that came from a salesperson.
- They should be text-based, not fancy HTML.
- State simply and clearly why you are reaching out.
- Make the email easy to read and respond to on a blackberry or smartphone.
- Offer credibility (e.g., examples of customers).
- Ask just one simple-to-answer question (such as for a referral).

And BE HONEST in all your communications, whether by phone or email.

One trick that I've seen reps use is to send an email to a new contact with a subject starting with "Re:" to make it look like they are responding to the prospect. Do you really want to start the relationship off with a lie? If you're a CEO or sales manager, don't allow or encourage anything that erodes integrity.

An Example Of What NOT To Write

Subject: Improve sales effectiveness in Q2?

Chuck,

> *Are you continually challenged to project accurate revenue?*
>
> *Do you know who your best reps are and what makes them successful?*
>
> *Do you know which marketing activities your company engages in are generating closed deals?*
>
> *You know there are some big deals in the pipeline, but can you easily generate a real-time report detailing their status?*

Does this sound familiar? You face the same challenges as many other companies. Salesforce.com has proven to be successful at leading global companies such as Adobe Systems, AOL Time Warner Communications, Putnam Lovell, Dow Jones Newswires, Berlitz Global Net, Siemens, Microstrategy and Autodesk, to name a few.

Salesforce.com is a web-based CRM service that can be rapidly rolled out and is easy to use. Sales organizations use it to centralize and report on contacts, accounts, and historical activities and to track sales performance. Marketing can easily measure the ROI of individual projects. Salesforce.com makes it very easy to customize reports and gain visibility into your sales organization and individuals' performance to get a better handle on your business.

Could we schedule 20 minutes of time to discuss this? Or would someone else in your organization be a more appropriate contact?

Warm regards, Aaron Ross

The above email is too long, impersonal, hard to read on a blackberry, sales-y and just uninteresting.

Response rate: ZERO.

Sending Your Campaigns

Start by sending 150-250 outbound emails per week, over the course of 3-4 days. Again, your goal is to receive an average of 5-10 responses per day, because if you get more than that, they will start dropping through the cracks. One of the biggest mistakes our clients make is sending too many emails per day.

Send the messages either before 9am or after 5pm, and avoid Mondays and Fridays. (Sundays are okay.)

If you are using emails, expect a 7-9%+ response rate (excluding bounces). This rate includes all responses: positive, negative and neutral.

For most newly built or purchased lists, you will get a 20-30% bounce rate – exclude those emails from your response rate calculation. So if you send 150 emails and receive 10 responses and 50 bounces, your response rate is 10% (10 responses / 100 valid emails).

Be methodical in how you handle responses! Response handling is critical to make sure no responses fall through the cracks. Log them and keep them organized. I suggest you create some standard email templates you can use for your most common responses.

Don't ignore bounces – clean bad emails out of your database as they come in. Over time they'll just clutter and fog up everything you do.

Learn to love "out of office" replies – those emails have the names and contact information for more people to target, such as executive assistants who job it is to help route you to the right person in the company!

Mass Email – So You Got A Response

First of all LOG EVERY RESPONSE into Salesforce.com (or your Sales Force Automation System), and update the contact as necessary. Once you begin doing high-volume prospecting, sending hundreds of emails per month, it's very easy to let great responses fall through the cracks.

The goal of every mass email should be to establish and close a prospect on a next step. That next step should be either one of two things—but NOT both:

- Who is the best point of contact for …?" (to get a referral); Or,
- When is the best day/time for a quick discussion around…?" (to set up a conversation with the prospect).

For goal #1, getting a referral, the objective is to confirm the best point of contact for a first conversation and get referred to them. Then, you can email the new contact (to whom you are referred) directly *while mentioning (or cc'ing) the individual who referred you.* This shows the new contact that you aren't making a cold call and you've already been engaged with someone from his or her team. Internal referrals create the highest likelihood of getting a response.

For goal #2, setting up a call, the objective is to set up a quick time to see if there's a high level fit between your company and the prospect's company. *This call should be focused entirely on their business – not your business.* You should lead the conversation and ask open questions that encourage them to talk about their business – not your business.

If you're talking more than 30% of the time on prospecting or scoping calls, you need to ask more questions or just keep your mouth shut more.

If someone responds with a negative, "Not interested", find out why.

Remember, "No" doesn't matter until you hear it from the CEO or your ideal decision maker. And even then when you get a No, you should find out why to determine if it's coming from an objection you can handle. Oftentimes prospects misunderstand what you do or what value you offer, and will say "no" out of confusion.

Contacts Who Didn't Respond

If somebody doesn't respond to your email, that doesn't mean there isn't legitimate potential in the account. By sending mass emails from Sales-force.com or another system that tracks "email opens," you can track which prospects opened your emails and how often they did it (or how many people they've passed your email to).

Here's an example:

Emails opened this week	
Name	Sum of # Times Opened
Chris Moloney	7
Andres Palcenuno	1
Jennifer Walker	1
Larry Wiseman	1
Megan Wertymer	1
Susan Riley	1
Todd Jones	1

Now, rather than having to randomly call prospects, you have a prioritized list of people to follow up with.

Review these reports every few hours. If someone's opened your email more than once, call them. If open rates are high, they might have forwarded the email to a few people.

Example "Old Opportunities" Campaign

A great place both to train new salespeople and generate opportunities is to reach back into old opportunities that have died, and have had no activity for at least six months.

Once a Sales Development Rep is trained and comfortable working with past leads, it will be easier for them to tackle totally cold accounts. Train them before you have them call on cold executives!

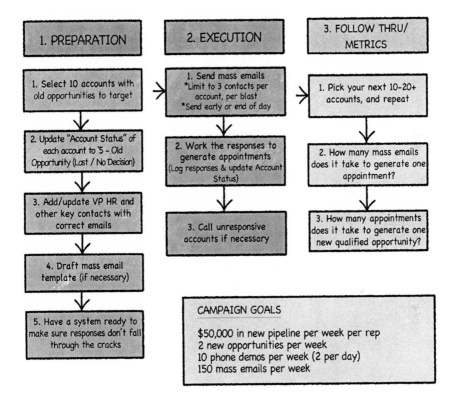

1. PREPARATION

1. Select 10 accounts with old opportunities to target

2. Update "Account Status" of each account to '5 - Old Opportunity (Lost / No Decision)

3. Add/update VP HR and other key contacts with correct emails

4. Draft mass email template (if necessary)

5. Have a system ready to make sure responses don't fall through the cracks

2. EXECUTION

1. Send mass emails
*Limit to 3 contacts per account, per blast
*Send early or end of day

2. Work the responses to generate appointments (Log responses & update Account Status)

3. Call unresponsive accounts if necessary

3. FOLLOW THRU/ METRICS

1. Pick your next 10-20+ accounts, and repeat

2. How many mass emails does it take to generate one appointment?

3. How many appointments does it take to generate one new qualified opportunity?

CAMPAIGN GOALS

$50,000 in new pipeline per week per rep
2 new opportunities per week
10 phone demos per week (2 per day)
150 mass emails per week

Sending Unsolicited Emails and CAN-SPAM Compliance

As a business, you can send unsolicited email messages to a newly acquired marketing list. If you use any kind of sales or marketing campaign with emails that are not "opt-in," such as purchased from a data service like Jigsaw or list broker, there are some rules you must follow to stay in compliance with CAN-SPAM, the anti-spam act.

You are allowed to send "unsolicited" emails to businesses. Here are the three core guidelines:

- The subject and header must not be misleading.
- You must have a valid physical address in your email.
- You must include a way to opt-out from future communications.

For more information, this page at the FTC has further guidance here:

http://www.ftc.gov/bcp/edu/pubs/business/ecommerce/bus61.shtm

Step 4: Sell The Dream

So one of your prospectors sets up time to have a full, first conversation with a prospect.

Assuming you are talking with a prospect who is a good fit for your service, the goal of "Selling The Dream" is NOT to "sell." It is, rather 1) to help the prospect create a vision of a dream solution that will solve their problems; and then 2) to connect your product to their key business issue(s) and dream solution.

In any conversation with a prospect, don't get eager until you actually see that they could be a fit. Challenge them as well. How serious are they about solving their challenges?:

- There's interest – but are they ready to take action?
- Are you connected with the people with power or influence?
- Is there real interest in a next step?

Outbound prospectors shouldn't just throw over lots of crummy opportunities that go nowhere – *it is better for them to pass fewer, better opportunities to your Account Executives.*

Track everything in your sales force automation system.

Once a prospector connects by phone with a prospect for a call to find out if there is a mutual fit, the biggest challenge is staying focused on the prospect's business and not selling yours.

Ask open-ended questions about their business first – how it's organized, for example – before moving on to ask about challenges.

Here are a series of sample questions you can customize and use in a Discovery Call. Realistically, in a first conversation a prospector might just ask 3-4 of these questions. They are roughly in order, starting with more general business questions and leading to more specific qualification questions:

- *How are your ____ teams/functions organized?*
- *How does your ____ process work today?*
- *What system(s) do these teams use for sales and lead management?*
- *How long has the system been in place?*

- *What are your challenges now? (After each answer, keep asking, "What else?")*
- *Have you been looking at alternatives yet?*
- *Have you tried and failed with other solutions? Why?*
- *Where does _____ fall on your priority list? What is higher?*
- *What would an ideal solution look like to you?*
- *How will your decision-making process work?*
- *Why did you buy the old system? Who made the decision to purchase it?*
- *What is the probability a project will occur this year [in the next six months]?*
- *Why do it now? (Or why wait until later?)*

More Tips For A First Call

- Main objective: get them talking about their business and then listen!!
- Call low before a C-level conversation: Find out how their business works and current challenges by calling a relevant employee at the company (at Salesforce.com, we'd call individual sales reps to get the inside scoop).
- Try being (respectfully) blunt: After you've talked, and if their pain isn't obvious, ask straight out if there is any pain: "Where do you have pain today? What's not working as well is it should?"
- Keep asking questions until you've exhausted the hunt for pain—their challenges. Keep digging until there's nothing left to uncover.
- Ask for referrals: Who else should you talk to at other divisions / teams?
- Scheduling via email is a huge time waster. Always work to schedule your next step while you're on the phone.

Remember, experiment and test these questions and practices to see what works for your people and business. You will have to customize, tweak and test to get great results that are repeatable.

Building Champions

If the prospect is interested but isn't ready, or they need to convince more people on the team, then turn your focus to developing your contact into a Champion, who can do the selling for you at the account.

It's simpler than you think: focus on what will make that person successful (not what will make you successful), and ask them how you can support them. Give them what they need – including time. Check in with them, but don't bug them. Build trust, be respectful, and be persistent.

You're planting seeds here, and it can take time for the seed to sprout and bloom. Keep "adding water" (giving them love and attention) and practicing patience with them!

Step 5: Pass The Baton (When Is An Opportunity Qualified?)

A question I get from every client is, "How do you define a qualified opportunity?" — that is, one which the inside Sales Development Rep (SDR) should pass to an Account Executive (AE), and that the SDR can be compensated on.

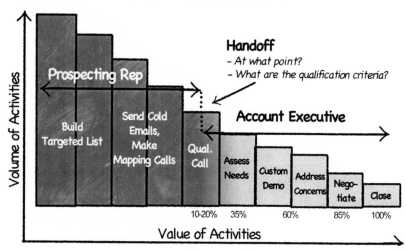

In this section, I'm going to be using the terms "Sales Development Rep" and "Account Executive" a lot, so while I'm not a fan of acronyms, I sometimes will use "SDR" and "AE" for brevity.

This process below was just for the outbound sales process. Salesforce. com had different qualification criteria for leads coming in through the website ("inbound leads"), which were routed to a totally different Market Response Reps team.

After lots of experimentation, these simple guidelines worked the best for our outbound generated opportunities....

The Basics

Apart from the qualification criteria, in order to be compensated for a new opportunity, the Sales Development Rep must find opportunities which:

- Have at least a potential of 20+ users (to ensure the sales reps were looking for large enough opportunities);
- Have no fundamental "red flags" or deal-breakers;
- The Sales Development Rep clearly generated (no poaching from "inbound" leads or other SDRs).

You must have clear guidelines and rules for reps to follow to help them ensure they are generating quality leads that are worth the company's time.

An all too common mistake is letting the pressure of "Just get leads in!" stop reps from disqualifying small deals that are not profitable enough. There is an opportunity cost to small deals – they waste time and resources that could be spent looking for or working on larger ones.

When An SDR Should Pass An Opportunity To An AE

Fundamentally, when the Sales Development Rep feels it is worth the Account Executive's time, that the Account Executive would want to engage this deal, they pass the opportunity over. There were three guidelines for this:

1. Does the company fit our ideal client profile?
2. Are we speaking with someone with influence or power?
3. Is there a clear interest in a next step, usually in the form of a scoping or discovery call with an Account Executive?

The opportunity is created and passed to the Account Executive still as a "Stage 1: New Prospect" opportunity. Even when passed to the Account Executive, it is not upgraded yet, and the Sales Development Rep is not compensated for it yet – not until it is re-qualified by the Account Executive.

How To Pass An Opportunity Smoothly

- *Best*: Hot-transfer the lead to the salesperson.
- *Okay*: Schedule a time on the calendars of your sales rep and the new lead for a discovery call.

- *Last option*: Make an email introduction, cc'ing both the sales rep and the new lead, with each other's contact information in the email.

And of course, the Sales Development Rep needs to log the email/pass in their sales force automation system, like Salesforce.com, and set up a new task or calendar item for their Account Executive.

The SDR Gets Credit *After* The Account Executive Re-qualifies

New opportunities are not upgraded to "qualified" until after the Account Executive speaks with and re-qualifies them in their own phone call. Do not let the Sales Development Rep get credit until this happens, it is so critical to quality control!

After the Account Executive speaks to the prospect on the phone and feels good about the same basic outbound qualification criteria *(Can we solve their problem? Are we in touch with the decision makers? Do they want a next step?...)*, the Account Executive can upgrade the opportunity to "Stage 2: Qualified".

Now the Sales Development Rep can get credit and compensated for it.

Use An Audit Process

It requires some extra time, but it is totally worth having a manager or the company owner review every single outbound opportunity to ensure high quality and integrity of the results.

As soon as an opportunity is upgraded, check it to ensure all of the following:

- Was this truly an incremental outbound opportunity? Not an inbound lead from your website?

- Was it re-qualified by the Account Executive by phone? (Sometimes an Account Executive would "do a favor" for their Sales Development Rep and upgrade opportunities before they re-qualified – a big no-no).

- Did the Sales Development Rep and Account Executive enter notes into your sales automation system appropriately? If it doesn't exist in your systems, it doesn't exist — and reps can't be compensated for it.

Back at Salesforce.com, the benefits of this strict auditing process, even though it took a little extra time and energy, were clear and solid:

- When I reported my results up the chain, including to Marc Benioff, I had total trust in the integrity of the data. I had rock-solid ROI proof of the team.

- The auditing forced the Sales Development Reps to step up the quality of their work, and reduced the temptation to push boundaries, such as poaching a lead from the inbound team.

It created trust within the team that everyone's results were fair and that no one was cheating.

Improve Call Effectiveness Without Scripts

Call scripts have been a classic tool in telemarketing and sales, but executives and business people have become much more tuned to canned questions. We use two simple but much more effective tools to plan and execute calls: AAA Call Planning and Call Flows.

AAA Call Planning

Even if a salesperson takes just five minutes, they can quickly generate a list of objectives for their call:

- What Answers do you want to learn in the call?
- What Attitudes do you wish the prospect to feel?
- What Actions should occur after the call?

Call Flows

The order of questions (how the conversation flows) makes a dramatic difference in the ease and productivity of calls. First, we reverse the classic cold call method that teaches salespeople to use the first 30 seconds to bark out an elevator pitch to spark a prospect's interest... because remember, we have already conversed via email or have a referral before we call.

So while the salesperson does want to begin with explaining why they are calling, and who they and their company are, it's not a cheesy "cold call pitch."

Salespeople should use a nonthreatening, research-oriented approach that uses the first half of the call to learn about the prospect's business and needs. The salesperson positions their service and value at the end of the call, after they've uncovered what the prospect actually wants. This means they position the solution to the specific needs of the prospect without lots of distracting, irrelevant information and features the prospect doesn't care about.

Below is a typical "flow" for a qualification call:

1. Opening ("Did I catch you at a bad time?") and Introduction
2. Discuss prospect's current business situation (authentic curiosity)

3. Probe for prospect's needs (and confirm understanding of the needs)

4. Position solution to meet those specific needs

5. Handle objections

6. Next steps

You don't need fancy scripts to help salespeople make effective calls. They can be useful during training, but don't let people get dependent on them and lose their own authentic voice.

Use more role-playing training and fewer scripts to teach them how to think on their feet and have more natural conversations.

Leaving Voicemails

Since email is the primary way people communicate today, use voicemail as a tool to increase response rates from emails rather than to attempt to get people to call you back (especially when targeting large companies; i.e., small business people are more likely to return voicemails).

Leave voicemails with the same demeanor you would use with a friend or family member. You want to be disarming and warm — not sales-y, sounding like a jackass or "corporate" (no personality). You should:

- State your name AND number at the beginning and end of the voicemail. This way, if they repeat the voicemail to get your phone number to call you back, they don't have to listen to it the whole way through to get to your number.

- Speak slowly and clearly. S-p-e-a-k s-l-o-w-l-y a-n-d c-l-e-a-r-l-y. Remember it can be hard to understand phone messages, especially if someone is calling into their messages through their cell phone.

- Explain in one or two sentences why you're calling them and at a minimum, imply a reason for why they should respond and how: "Responding to your email," "Saw you visited our website," "Wanted to ask for the courtesy of a response to the email I sent you"....

- Say their name at least twice, as people love hearing their own name, and it's rapport-building.

If you haven't sent them an email yet, send an email as soon as you leave them the voicemail – give them more than one way to get back to you.

- **Example 1**: *"Hi John, this is Aaron Ross from Salesforce.com. My number is 555-555-5555. John, I sent you an email a couple of days ago and hadn't heard back, and I was hoping you could give me a quick courtesy response. I'll resend it here in a minute. Again, Aaron Ross, 555-555-5555. Thank you and have a great day."*

- **Example 2**: *"Hi John, this is Aaron Ross from Salesforce.com. My number is 555-555-5555. John, I'm calling to follow up on the email I sent you, I'd love to hear either way if you can please help me out or not. Again, Aaron Ross, 555-555-5555. Thank you and have a great day."*

- **Example 3** (the mysterious version): *"Hi John, this is Aaron Ross following up. My number is 555-555-5555. I'm free after 3pm today. Again, Aaron Ross, from Salesforce.com, 555-555-5555. Thanks and have a great day."*

The last message is likely to get you the highest callback rate, since it is mysterious. I'm not a fan of this last message with new prospects because they can call you back thinking it's something important only to find out "Oh it's a salesperson," and leaving a bad taste in their mouth. I suggest using it with people you've already had contact with who could or should recognize your name.

Voicemail can be effective in combination with email. When people do call you back directly, they'll often say things like, "I wasn't going to call you back at first, but you were so persistent..." or, "Thanks for the reminder, I've been meaning to call you back...."

Voicemail can be effective in combination with email.

Voicemail also lets them hear your voice and helps establish that you're a real human, which is why it's important not to get too mechanical with scripts and lose the humanity in your voice.

Move Prospects Through "Account Status" Assembly Line Stages

You can't predictably create revenue without predictable pipeline, and that requires ways to measure and track how pipeline gets created.

An effective, easy-to-use sales automation or CRM system makes it convenient now to use a simple idea, the assembly line, as a model to "manufacture new pipeline", implying a sales organization that can measurably, consistently and predictably produce new sales opportunities.

Just as you use stages in your sales process to track movement and progress through it, you need similar stages in your prospecting process.

Also, if you can establish specific actions and methods for dealing with a prospect depending on which specific stage they are in, you will be far more effective as a salesperson. Our analogous sales process system for prospecting stages is called "Account Status."

These stages are separate and complementary to your sales process stages, because they precede the creation of a new sales opportunity.

Below are the assembly line stages you should use to track how you're moving prospects through your prospecting process (customize as you see fit):

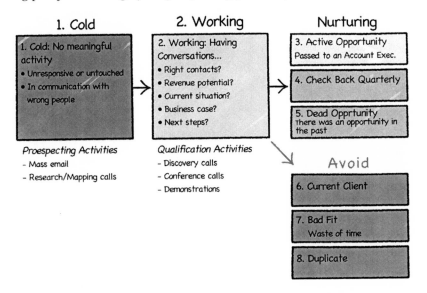

These "Account Status" settings are the equivalent of sales stages in opportunities, but specifically for accounts/organizations. So the account is "cold," the account is "working," and so on.

It is essential for reps (especially Sales Development Reps who are prospecting for new business) to be able to organize their accounts in this manner so that reps can focus on the right accounts with the right messages at the right time, and minimize wasted efforts.

It's highly embarrassing for your outbound sales team to be sending prospecting emails or making prospecting calls into your current customers!

How To Use These Stages

Create a new data field in your sales system on the Accounts/Organizations page or tab called "Account Status," which is a pick list. Add these eight settings. Test them out and feel free to customize them to your own language and process.

Here are further explanations for the statuses, which you can also think of "Bins" where you put accounts:

Bin: 1. Cold

This should be pretty self-evident, but it's accounts where you have no activity, and no real insight into whether they're a fit or not. Often this bucket consists of data you've imported from someplace like Jigsaw and unresponsive accounts.

Bin: 2. Working

This bucket includes all the prospects that a rep is actively touching and researching. A rep has some kind of conversation going on at this account, either by email or phone. They may not be sure if the company is a good prospect yet, if there's interest, or even who the right influencers are.

The goal of a rep with an account in the "Working" status is NOT to generate a sales opportunity by any means necessary. The primary goal is to determine the "truth" of whether there is, or is not, an opportunity at this account in the next several weeks or months. If there isn't, it's better to move on than to generate a poor opportunity that will distract sales reps from "real" ones.

"Nurture" Bin: 3. Active Opportunity

When a rep generates a new sales opportunity and that opportunity is still alive, use this status to remove that account from the assembly line. For Sales Development Reps, it makes it easy to check on the accounts and opportunities they've passed to their sales rep partners, to make sure no batons got dropped (which happens more than you'd like).

"Nurture" Bin: 4. Check Back Quarterly

I like status names that speak for themselves :) There's no current opportunity here, but there should be someday.

"Nurture" Bin: 5. Dead Opportunity

Accounts with a dead sales opportunity are special, and deserve their own category, because they are highly likely to become customers in the future.

"Avoid" Bin: 6. Current Client

Small companies may not "get" this, but trust me: As your customer base gets bigger, and the data in your SFA/CRM system gets messier, it's almost impossible to keep your Sales Development Reps from calling on current customers. You want to make sure the team prospecting into cold accounts avoids current customers, and this is a way to help them do that.

"Avoid" Bin: 7. Bad Fit

No business fit, or perhaps they're out of business. It's a waste of time to ever talk to this company.

"Avoid" Bin: 8. Duplicate Account

Sometimes you don't want to delete an account or lead. By marking it duplicate, you can make sure you avoid it in the future.

SDR Compensation

I experimented quite a bit with different compensation structures at Salesforce.com. The best was the simplest with just two components:

A Base salary: $_____

A Commission of $_____ (targeted to be about 50% of the base, or 1/3 of their total)

Depending on where you are in the country, your base, for a quality person, could range from $35,000–$60,000, and the commission could range from $20,000–$60,000.

The low end compensation would be if you're hiring new college graduates, and selling goods with smaller orders – several thousand to $15,000 dollars.

The higher compensations are if you're hiring people with 5 years experience who are selling premium business-to-business services that cost at least $50,000.

Commission Structure

The commission is paid monthly. It is made up of two parts:

- 50% depends on a goal for the number of qualified opportunities generated this month.
- 50% is paid based on deals that close, such as a percentage of revenue.

This structure balances short- and long-term goals. It incents Sales Development Reps to generate many opportunities now, while encouraging them also to focus on the size of deals and likelihood of closing.

SDRs: Account Executives Are Your Customers

Your job as a salesperson is to establish such value with your customers that they tell everyone they know how good you are and what a fantastic job you've done. This is true whether you are a company or an individual.

As an SDR, your customers are the Account Executives you support and work with. Make them successful, and they will make you successful.

Your customers are always your greatest assets.

Example Simplified Training Plan For A New SDR

Assumption: The first 2-4 weeks of their job are focused on general company training, product training, services, etc., before they focus on SDR training.

Week 3

Every day: 3 Goals *(see examples on the next page)*

1. Daily training
2. Configure Salesforce.com, explore Salesforce.com
3. Sit with an SDR and salesperson every day
4. Add an account and contacts from your source of data
5. Learn how to de-duplicate accounts (how to thoroughly check new leads to ensure they are not already in the system)
6. Send a mass outbound email to 20-50 contacts
7. Transition the prior SDR's territory

Weeks 4 and 5

Every day: 3 Goals *(see examples on the next page)*

1. Send 100 outbound emails before Friday
2. Practice logging and responding to emails correctly
3. Work up to five "call conversations" per day by the end of the week
4. Have a veteran SDR sit with you every day
5. Draft a personal dashboard
6. Discuss a new section of the training materials with the team

Sample Beginning Daily Goals

- Pick a new online Salesforce.com training module to study
- Call five old (not cold) leads in the system, to practice discussing their needs in a business conversation
- "Ideal Customer Profile" discussion with teammate
- Learn about the "Account Status" stages
- Add five new accounts and their contacts into Salesforce.com
- Send a mass email
- Meet with a mentor
- Meet someone from another team
- Listen to a sales call
- Listen to a prospecting call
- Draft your "Day in the Life"

Sample Intermediate Daily Goals

- Configure Salesforce.com reports or a dashboard
- Customize your own Cheat Sheet
- Practice "Mapping Calls" into cold accounts (call the executive assistant of the President, and ask for a referral to the right contact)
- Role play some calls with a teammate
- Large account mapping project (pick a Fortune 1000 account and map out 3-5 divisions)
- Draft your plan for the month – Vision? Methods? Metrics?
- Business Problems v. Business Solutions role-play exercise
- Run a "Dead Opportunities" campaign into accounts with old opportunities

Remember again, you will have to experiment, test and measure to figure out what works and is repeatable for your business and team. If something doesn't work the first time, keep tweaking!

4

Prospecting and Sales Best Practices

*A collection of tips and tricks that any salesperson
can use to improve results.*

A "Day in the Life" (SDR Example)

How intentional are you in designing your day, or the days of your sales-people? Here is an example of an "ideal day" in the life of a Sales Development Rep. You can take the principles behind it and design your own "ideal day" templates for other roles in your company.

"Day In A Life" of a "Sales Development Rep" (Full-time)	
MY 3 GOALS TODAY:	1)
	2)
	3)
Examples of daily goals: "Get 5 call conversations", "schedule 2 appointments", "complete and send a proposal", "import 10 new accounts", "send 50 mass emails", "update my dashboard"...	
When you first get in	Plan the day - what do you want to accomplish today?
7:30 - 8:30 AM	Handle hot email responses / tasks
8:30 AM - 8:45 AM	Personal
8:45 AM - 9 AM	Plan a calling session - targets and goals
9:00 - 11:00 AM	Calling Session - goal is 5 "Call Conversations"

Free gift: download this "Day In The Life Template" from:
www.PredictableRevenue.com/templates

In this case, the first half of the day is primarily for following up on new and past leads, although perhaps the most important five minutes is in the beginning, when the SDR considers their "3 goals for the day".

In summary, the most effective days begin with prioritizing key goals for the day, then a morning of responding to leads ("important and urgent" work), and and afternoon of calls and preparation for the future ("important, not urgent" work).

After lunch, the day is blocked out to focus on scheduled calls and demos and planning. Lastly, the SDR sends out an evening email campaign so that they have fresh responses waiting in their inbox in the morning.

1:00 - 1:30 PM	
1:30 PM - 2:00 PM	
2:00 PM - 3:00 PM	
3:00 PM - 3:30 PM	
3:30 PM - 4:00 PM	Personal
4:00 PM - end of day	Prepare to send your mass emails
End of day	Review open tasks, make sure no important ones slip through the cracks
Before leaving	Send mass emails (50)

Maintaining Enthusiasm

Finally, to maintain sustainable and positive sales energy in the team, it's important for sales reps to take breaks every 90 minutes, take a full lunch with coworkers, and pick a time of day to commit to stopping work (such as 6pm). Overwork can produce more results in the short-term, but will eventually grind out anyone's "authentic enthusiasm" and create burn out and turnover in the team.

The Top Six Prospecting Mistakes Reps Make

1. Expecting Instant Results

When targeting companies that have multiple people involved in decisions (often a couple hundred employees and up), it can take 2-4 weeks, or longer, just to develop a new qualified opportunity.

2. Writing Long Emails

Long emails can be hard to process – especially when so many people read them on mobile phones. Can someone read and respond easily to your email on a Blackberry? Make it easy for them to respond by asking them a single simple question.

Also in email (or by phone), state simply why you are reaching out – and be honest! You really don't need to be tricky. The truth is the most persuasive form of marketing.

3. Going Wide, Not Deep

Hitting 100 accounts once instead of 10 accounts 10 times each.

4. Giving Up Too Quickly At Ideal Targets

Don't give up on working to understand if there is a fit or not until you get a "no" from the real decision maker. Be "pleasantly persistent."

5. Not Giving Up Quickly Enough At Non-Ideal Targets

Persistence is valuable, but is a double-edged sword. Being persistent with prospects that aren't a good fit is a waste of time.

6. Depending On Activity Metrics Rather Than A Proven Process

"Dials per day" isn't nearly as useful as tracking "call conversations per day" or "appointments per week". What's your step-by-step process and waterfall? Measure results that are proven to lead to revenue rather than throwing lots of activity at a goal.

My Favorite Prospecting Questions

Here are my personal favorite sales questions to open and start great conversations with people you don't know:

- "Did I catch you at a bad time?"

This is my all-time favorite question for opening any conversation. In fact, I have a whole page about it a bit later here in the book.

By asking "did I catch you at a bad time," you are showing your respect for their time by asking permission to chat. It takes them off the defensive. It demonstrates that you're not a sales jackass.

More often than not, they'll say, "It's not a good time, but how can I help you?"...and then go ahead and chat with you for 10-15 minutes!

- May I ask how your [sales teams | marketing organization | research efforts...] is organized?

People like to talk about their business. It's harder to begin with a "What are your top challenges?" question, because a) they don't trust you yet, and b) they may not have thought about their challenges. Give them an easy question to answer, such as, "May I ask how your marketing organization (search engine efforts, recruiting process, etc.) is structured?"

Using an open-ended question encourages them to talk about it and get warmed up, to start thinking of challenges. Also, sharing the structure or process of a part of their business will be easy for them (not requiring much thinking), and will give you excellent situational information on their business.

This is an excellent follow-up question after you tell them, honestly and directly, why you're calling ("I'm doing some research on your company to determine if we're a fit or not...").

- If you were me, how would you approach your organization?

A great question after you've talked with someone who's helpful, but not the right person at that company.

- Do you have your calendar handy?

Never schedule by email if you can help it. Get on the calendar (whether it's for yourself or you're setting an appointment up for someone else) right there while you're on the phone!

7 Quick Prospecting Tricks

1. **Call/Email High**: Rather than going directly to your target, call above them and get referred down to the right person.

2. **Attitude**: You're a non-threatening researcher, not a pushy salesperson.

   Favorite Questions (useful by phone or email):

   - (Phone only): "Did I catch you at a bad time?"
   - "Who is the right person to talk to about _____?"
   - "May I ask how your ___ [team/process/function] [is structured/works] today?"
   - "Would it be a waste of time to discuss _____ to see if we could help?"

3. **Think "Bite-sized Emails"**:

   - Keep it short and sweet! Assume emails are read on Blackberries.
   - Ask one (and only one) question per email... keep it simple.

4. **If They Aren't Interested, Find Out Why**:

   - Is (whatever problem you solve) just not a priority? No budget? Organizational change has the place in chaos right now?
   - Is it worth your time to dig more, or should you move on?
   - This insight is important because you will learn if the blocks are objections to overcome, or what and when your next step should be.

5. **Don't Give Up Too Easily! (With Ideal Prospects)**:

   - With ideal prospects, don't disqualify them until you get a "no" from the decision maker (don't take "no" from others, even other executives). If you sell to the VP Sales and feel the account is ideal, don't assume that because the CIO says you're wasting your time that you are.

   As Winston Churchill said, "Never, never, never, never give up!" (with ideal prospects).

6. Always Set Up a Next Step

- What next step will both help your process and create value
  for the prospect? Always frame a next step in a way that
  is valuable to them: "The best way for us to save time...";
  "Here's how I can help you get to a decision faster...";
  "Your team will learn...."

- About one out of four prospects will have had a strong
  opinion on the next step they wanted to take. In that case
  they'll often say, "I need to see a demo." If you have a
  different idea about what you want, don't fight them. Take
  their next step with them, and "enhance" their idea with
  what you want: "I'd be happy to set up a demo. As part
  of that preparation process, it'll help make our time much
  more productive if you fill out these five questions...."

- The other 75% of prospects will look to you to suggest
  the best next step. You're there to walk them through an
  evaluation and buying process. So be prepared to have
  one or two specific suggestions based on what's been most
  efficient for your other clients: "What we've found as a
  best next step is to..."

Try out these tips, and keep track of your own "few, best practices and
questions" that work in your market. Put them into a cheat sheet that
you can use in training new sales reps and helping veterans prepare for
sales calls.

Time Management and Focus Tip: "3 Goals For The Day"

One of my favorite time management practices – one that works for any sales rep or CEO – is to map out three-to-five main goals for the coming day. I like doing it the night before.

Ask yourself, "If I could only get three things done today, what would they be?" It's harder than you think to get three important things done!

Examples of sales daily goals (keep them simple):

- Have *and log* five phone conversations.
- Send a campaign of 150 mass emails.
- Qualify a new sales opportunity.
- Schedule two Scoping/Discovery Calls.
- Map out a success plan (goals, activities, methods) for next month.

For a great online application now that helps you prioritize your daily, weekly, monthly and quarterly goals, take a look at www.Teamly.com.

**Example 1-Page
Printed Template**

3 Goals For Today:

3 Goals For Today:

Free gift: download this "3 Goals Template" from:
www.PredictableRevenue.com/templates

3 Goals For Today:

Example Dashboards In Salesforce.com

For A Sales Team

I encourage clients to generally set up their dashboards in a three column format, including:

- Left: Current month activity (amount of stuff going on).

- Center: current month results/deals.

- Right: Long-term results (year-to-date).

Example screenshot, blurred for privacy:

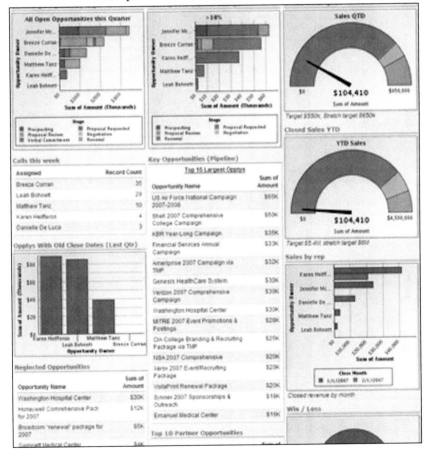

Example Sales Development Rep Dashboard

Every sales rep should set up their own personal dashboard, so they can see the state of their own business at a glance (and it makes it easier for their manager to coach/help them).

Below, I have laid out a three-column dashboard with nine example reports, in a 3x3 matrix. Notice how the reports follow the same three-column format I suggested on the prior page.

- Left: Current month activity (amount of stuff going on).
- Center: current month results/deals.
- Right: Long-term results (year-to-date).

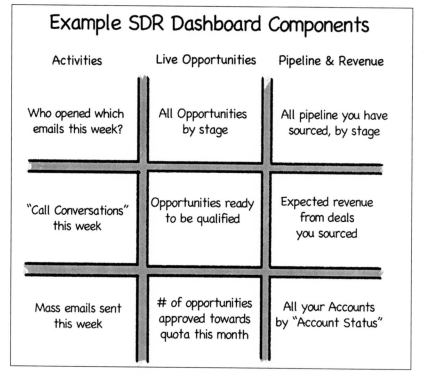

Example SDR Dashboard Components

Activities	Live Opportunities	Pipeline & Revenue
Who opened which emails this week?	All Opportunities by stage	All pipeline you have sourced, by stage
"Call Conversations" this week	Opportunities ready to be qualified	Expected revenue from deals you sourced
Mass emails sent this week	# of opportunities approved towards quota this month	All your Accounts by "Account Status"

Every team is different, and while for outbound sales you should use the above key metrics and reports as a foundation, you will have to customize everything to fit your own needs.

5

Sales Best Practices

Shorten sales cycles. Increase sales productivity.

Sell To Success

Selling the Predictable Revenue way is about "Selling To Success." It's about hiring and training salespeople who are totally committed to their company's vision and values. It's salespeople helping new prospects connect with that vision, and then helping these new customers succeed — and generating lots of revenue as a byproduct.

These salespeople don't close customers that aren't a good long-term fit. They work with a team of other great salespeople, all helping each other improve and learn as a team. Compensation is important, but it's not the most important thing.

Traditional "ABC" Selling

People from old school sales mindsets live by "Always Be Closing!" They destructively compete with coworkers. They close wrong-fit customers. They sell just to get paid, and that's almost the only reason they stay in the job. "ABC Selling" skips two essential steps: creating a Success Plan before negotiating an agreement, and focusing on Ongoing Customer Success after the close.

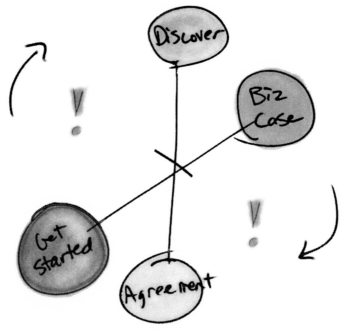

What Makes "Closing" So Artificial

Salespeople get paid to close deals, and they tend to be pressured — I mean managed — by fear. Fear is the conventional sales management tool of choice.

Ever seen the Glengarry Glen Ross "Always Be Closing!" sales motivation speech? It's extreme, but there are grains of truth in there.

When anyone gets paid to do something, and has managers breathing down their neck, it distorts behavior. Empathy with prospects is lost in the push to "Just close the deal!" Trusting, capable managers can help protect their salespeople from these distorting effects by focusing on doing the right thing; fear-driving managers exacerbate the problem.

The result: powerful incentives to sell high-value services like a late night cable TV guy. "Buy now and get a month-end discount!" (By the way, to prospects getting time pressured: Don't you realize you can get the same discount next month?)

Is the high pressure you're applying today generating short-term results at the expense of long-term results or client/employee trust?

What Customers Care About (And It Ain't Your Sale)

Customers don't care at all whether you close the deal or not. They care about improving their business. It's easy to forget this in the heat of a sales cycle.

Okay, yes, you know that – but do you live it? Do you remember it? You or your team probably isn't selling this way.

This idea is constantly driven out of salespeople's heads by the pressure of commissions, quotas and stress. Reminding them (and their managers) requires constant reinforcement.

Sell Past The Close With A "Success Plan"

Sell "past the close" to the prospect's own vision of their success – however they define it. Help them define it for themselves. Success is not when your service is launched; it's when your service is successfully impacting the customer's business, such as when your software is adopted (not just deployed).

Push Selling vs. Pull Selling

A benefit of selling this way is to begin to pull prospects through a buying cycle, rather than pushing them through a sales cycle. Not only is it a pain to push a prospect through a sales cycle, it tends to be a lot less productive, and you end up with more customers who aren't a great long-term fit for the company.

Selling to success helps pull a prospect through a buying cycle by helping tie their goals and desires to your company's ability to help achieve their goals.

The Trick

One of the tricks in "selling to success" is to not care too much about the close. Caring too much about the close will cause you to give off subconscious signals to the customer that you really don't care about their success, you care more about getting paid or getting your manager off your back.

That's the irony of stressing too much about the close itself: the stress can reduce the likelihood of it happening.

The Close Becomes A Natural Step In Achieving The Vision

If you and the customer create a joint vision around how your company will make them successful, and they believe you, then the close becomes just a logical step in the progression to achieve that dream. You can remove the artificiality of "closing," and make it feel natural.

Two Steps To Help Your Team Sell To Success

First: Include a SIMPLE "Success Plan" step before you close. This is a plan (almost a vision) that paints a picture of the basic steps beyond deployment to actual client success. It should also include a definition of what success means to the client, a few key milestones, and some responsibilities of both your company and the client.

This "plan" can literally be a half dozen bullet points in an email, agreed on with the client. It should be simple enough so that anyone at the client company who sees it will quickly grasp its essence and vision. Do not create a complex plan.

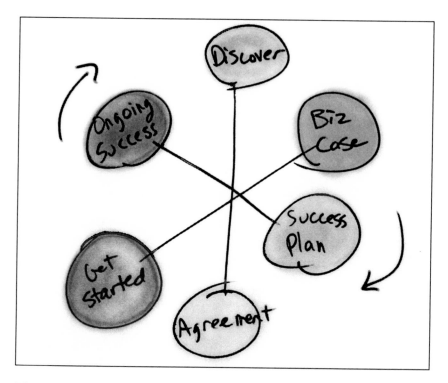

The more clear the client's vision of their success, the more they'll want to pull the deal forward on their own.

Second: What is your plan for a client's ongoing success? Do you have a role in your company dedicated solely to helping customers become successful in using your product or service? It's easy to want to push all the responsibility for success onto the customer, but it is equally your responsibility to help them succeed, because happy customers will help your business. It's both the right and the profitable thing to do.

9 Ways You Lengthen Your Sales Cycles

A never-ending goal of companies is, "How can we shorten sales cycles?" There are no silver bullets. But there are some patterns around what lengthens cycles and how to shorten them.

While I could come up with a million-and-one issues that delay cycles, here are the eight main ones to look into first.

1) Wrong Prospects, Poor Messaging (Square Peg / Round Hole)

It takes longer than you want to nail your market and messaging. Companies sell to the wrong people and companies ALL THE TIME. Or they sell to the right people with language that sounds good and fancy to investors, but means nothing to prospects ("We are the leading social graph platform integration appliance blah blah blah....")

It's human nature – you want more customers, and you get desperate anytime anyone gives you a sign of interest. (I'll refrain from making the so-obvious dating analogy here.)

"Pick a niche, get rich." If your marketing and sales efforts aren't focused on your Ideal Customers, you will spend way too much time and energy on prospects who don't really need what you have to offer (or they don't understand yet why they need it).

2) No Sales Process

Do you have a sales process? If you don't – get one. ANYTHING is better than no process. A consistent process that isn't working well is better than no process, because you can improve consistent systems – you can't improve random systems.

3) You Have A Fantastic But Unused Sales Process

You have a great sales process but still struggle. Do your reps actually follow the process? Is it simple? (Complexity reduces adoption). How is it supposed to work in the trenches? Have you customized the process to your specific business? When was the last time you sat down with a rep or reps and watched or listened or asked about what they really do each day, and how effective it is?

4) "Selling Selfishly" Rather Than "Solving"

Are your reps just pushing deals and "selling," or are they proving to the clients that they can help solve problems? Do your reps disqualify? (Reps that just "sell sell sell" don't disqualify enough). Can reps, as described in the prior section on "Selling To Success," create a clear vision that empowers and pulls clients into really wanting what you have to offer?

5) Selling Too Low

Find out early who has influence and approval power – who's involved in the sale? Yes, I know, this isn't revolutionary – but reps don't do this. REPS DO NOT DO THIS. They are afraid to ask because they're intimidated by executives and they're afraid bold questions will derail their deal. Sales reps tend to spend time with the people at a prospect that are willing to spend time with them (it's easier).

- In pipeline reviews or one-on-one coaching sessions, be merciless in finding out how much energy reps are putting into mapping out decision-making processes and people.

- If they aren't directly in touch with decision makers, how can they help their Champion or main point of contact sell for them? (Never assume your internal champion knows how to or can sell internally for you!)

- When doing outbound sales, start high – one or two levels higher than your decision maker.

- Have reps practice role-playing with people at your company that can think and speak like decision-makers. It will give the reps confidence, and teach them how to have better conversations with senior people.

- How can you position your product and marketing to resonate and sell higher?

6) Poor Understanding Of The Prospect's Buying Process (Or What It Takes To Close This Deal)

Ask the prospects how their buying process works. Every company has their own buying quirks. Don't be afraid to probe. The better you understand how their process works, the more effectively you can help them figure out if your product is a fit or not.

If your prospect (or market) has an average six-month buying process, there's no point in getting impatient at month three.

- What's your usual process to evaluate and buy products like this?"
- What would it take to close in [30/60/90] days? (Or by a certain date)
- How can we get this done?" (Later in a sales cycle)

When asking bold questions, it's not what you ask, it's how you ask it. If you ask a question like, "How can we get this done?" in an insecure way, it will hurt you. Ask it easily and confidently, and it can close the deal for you.

7) Not Caring About Them

Do you really want to help them improve their business, or just sell them stuff? Great salespeople focus on making their prospects successful. How can you help your prospects, even if there's no direct connection to a sale yet? Are their resources, news, advice, referrals or other things of value you can share with them? When you call, do you authentically care about how their business is going, or are you just focused on finding out if they're ready to buy yet? Focusing on their success builds trust, which leads to more sales.

8) Telling Instead Of Showing (How Can You Prove It?)

If you're still working on breaking into an account, or have a stagnant prospect, try giving them something for free that will be valuable to them, like a free trial. Instead of telling them how great you are, or what a leader your company is, how can you prove it? For example, a trial can create a first point of entry in the "getting to know you" stage and give buyers a taste that you have the credibility to help them. Don't just throw free stuff at them. Tailor what you're offering to whatever their needs or problems are, or else it's likely to be a waste of time for both parties.

9) Dragging Your Feet In Disqualifying

I love Tom Batchelder's book titled Barking Up A Dead Horse (and I recommend it!). Because of desperation, pressure or a lack of clarity on their "Ideal Customer Profile," executives and salespeople will beat dead or poor-fit opportunities to death, simply because that opportunity is in front of them, and it's easier to whip it than to go looking for new ones. Every month, go in and clear your pipeline clutter to create space for new, high quality opportunities!

Obsess About the Decision Making Process, Not The Decision Maker

In the past, Sales was ALL about the decision maker, and everyone else on their team wasn't thought of as important.

Now, because executives are busier than ever, and because business culture is more collaborative and less dictatorial, decision makers rely more and more on their teams to help them make purchase decisions.

In the past, when decision makers would defer salespeople to their subordinates, it was because the decision maker didn't think it was important or valuable, and wanted to blow salespeople off.

Salespeople were rightly trained to fight to get around this objection and obtain the decision makers' time no matter what.

Now, the "decision making process" is more important than "the decision maker."

Avoid questions like:

> "Who is the decision maker?"

> "Who signs the check?"

Ask questions like:

> "How have you evaluated similar products or services?"

> "What is the decision making process?"

> "Who is involved in making the decision?"

> "How will the decision be made?"

> "What are the steps to have a check cut or funds released?"

Now, when a decision maker refers you to their "get it done" people (the influencers), it's a perfectly good way to begin selling into an account.

Should you ignore decision makers early on? No!

In other words, sales reps shouldn't wimp out and avoid trying to build a relationship with the decision maker, but it's not always urgent to get there from the beginning (though it is a big help).

Is reaching the ultimate decision makers any less important? No!

Win over your internal champions and coaches first; build the case. Then you'll be perfectly positioned to win over the final decision makers.

You do want to build a relationship with the decision makers early, but don't "sell" them until you've begun winning over the influencers, or at least until they've begun to agree with the value of your business case. Build some credibility and understanding of the business first.

You'll look weak, lame or 'sales-y' if you're pitching a business case to the decision maker that their influencers disagree with or don't fully buy into yet.

Finally, when a salesperson doesn't understand the decision-making process (which is all too common!), there's a lot less visibility into how long the sale can take, the likelihood of closing, and hidden landmines.

Busy salespeople tend not to ask enough (or bold enough) questions of prospects around how the prospect's internal processes work.

If you're a salesperson: With your current top five deals, how well have you mapped out their internal buying process?

If you're a sales executive: If you sat down with your team and had them talk about their own top deals, how clear are they, not just on the current status of the deal or the next step, but also the prospect's actual internal process to get to a decision?

9 Steps To Create Free Trials That Maximize Conversion Rates

These principles are written for sales rep-driven free trials (where the reps are coordinating and negotiating the free trial as part of a sales cycle), but you can also apply the principles to online self-managed trials.

1. Design The Trial With Your Prospect (And Help Them Run It)

You'll see this as a theme in all the following points. Don't just throw or push a trial on a prospect. Instead, how can you enroll them in wanting it, defining success, running it and growing it? You have to help them make it successful. Help them help themselves.

2. Do Your Best To Understand The Prospect's True Business Issues Before You Begin

Sounds like a no-brainer, right? Except that reps are so eager to jump into a demo or get a free trial going that they frequently don't prepare enough. Also, prospects frequently aren't very clear on what they want – especially if you're dealing with multiple influencers and users. Without the homework of really understanding their challenges and desires, you can't begin with the end in mind and design the trial for success.

3. Agree With The Prospect On Where The Free Trial Fits In Their Buying Process (Or Your Selling Process)

A free trial is just one part of a longer (but hopefully not too much longer!) sales or buying cycle. If the trial is successful, then what? Answer that question before you begin the trial.

4. Better To Nail Fewer (Or A Single) Key Problems Than Try To Solve Every Problem For Everyone

The trial will only be a success if the prospect gets value and knows it. Everyone is busy, so pick your battle. Where can you show the biggest bang-for-the-buck? (In this case, "buck" means the prospect's time and attention.) What would be the easiest place to prove success? Build fast wins early and then add features over time. "If we could only solve 1-3 things with this trial, what would they be?"

5. Define With The Client What A "Successful Trial" Means

How will the client (including the decision maker) know the trial is a success? Map this out with the client before you begin. Don't be afraid to ask the client questions like, "What does success look like? What do we [you and the prospect] need to accomplish with the trial before you want to move forward with us?"

6. Create Milestones For The Trial

Lay out a plan with regular milestones. Hitting milestones creates momentum and creates more proof of value. Keep them simple, such as "80% of users take training in Week 1"; "Three executive dashboards built"; or, "50 leads generated and accepted." Don't be afraid to update or change milestones along the way. Always have a next goal or milestone for the prospect to be working towards!

7. Enroll The Prospect (And Their Team)

Just because a prospect agrees to do a free trial and makes a plan doesn't mean they are going to follow through – especially if your contact hasn't sold their internal people on it yet. Make sure the customer has the right expectations of how much time and effort they need to put into the trial to make it succeed. Tip: have them pre-schedule time or activities (including check-ins with you) into their calendar for a few weeks in advance: "Let's schedule this now, so that you don't have to worry about it later."

8. Simplify The Trial Process

How can you make the trial as simple and easy as possible for the client? Do you have a step-by-step system, instructions or training for them? Don't make them think. Paralysis comes with complexity. Make it as simple as you can for them to succeed.

9. Set Expectations

Most success comes from expectations – did you over-promise and under-deliver? Or vice versa? Expectations are incredibly powerful, and can make or break trust with your prospect… and hence the sale.

A 3-Hour-and-15-Minute Sales Process

Just as important as sales cycle length is *how many hours of selling time per rep does each sales cycle require?* How can they be much more efficient and effective, in order to handle more deals with higher close rates?

Reps tend to waste a LOT of time chasing early and stalled deals *("Hi Bob, just checking in to see if anything's changed yet over there. It hasn't? OK, I'll call you again in two weeks...")*

Also, Bob here in the example might be someone without much power or influence, and no matter how long the rep persists, nothing's ever going to happen.

My "3-Hour-and-15-Minute" Sales Process is a big help in the early stages of a sales cycle to qualify it, get access to decision makers and build a common vision. It's also very simple. I developed it when I began doing sales consulting, to minimize the amount of time both parties needed to figure out whether or not we should work together, and when.

The objectives of this process are to qualify or disqualify early, gain access to the multiple people in a deal that have power, and begin creating a common vision with the prospect.

There are three steps that add up to three hours and fifteen minutes of total time invested to get to the point that *both parties know there's a good fit and when is the right time to engage (even if that is not today).*

Step 1: (15 Minutes) First Contact: *"Is This A Waste Of Time?"*

Imagine you are referred to someone, or get a response from a prospect and have a first chat with them. You can take fifteen minutes with them to figure out whether or not it's a waste of time to speak further.

Frankly, everyone's so busy and overwhelmed these days that they appreciate being told what to do, so that they don't have to think. In this first call, start setting expectations right away. Lay out your process for the prospect in the best way to mutually figure out the fit, and position it in a way that benefits them.

"We've found the best way to quickly figure out if there's a real fit or not takes just two steps: first, a more in-depth 'discovery' call with yourself and any other people you want to bring in. And then if that call goes well, a follow-up group whiteboarding session or call with the key people on your team who'd be involved, so that we can flesh it out all at once if, how and when we should work together."

Step 2: (One Hour) Qualification / Discovery Call: *"Is There A Fit?"*

This is a call with one or two of the prospect's point people, the ones that usually check out new vendors. They want see if they like you and what you're doing enough to spend more time on your company and introduce you to more people involved in their evaluation.

You are qualifying or disqualifying them as well – remember, if it's not a good fit, you should move on!

Your goal, if there is a fit, is to create a plan with the prospect to organize a working or whiteboarding session that brings in their key people and decision makers, to meet with and create a vision with your key people.

It's not always realistic to do this with every prospect, but it isn't as hard as you might think. The more confidently you can lay out your process, and why it works for them, too (which it does!), the more likely they'll follow along.

Do they really want you bugging them for months about whether there's a fit? Why not just figure it out now?

Step 3: (Two Hours) Group Working Session: *"Should We Work Together?"*

In this session, you want to create a joint vision together. Walk them through a design process on how they can and will become successful with your product. *Coach* the vision out of them rather than telling it to them.

It's fine to use slides for introductions and to set the context, but move to whiteboards quickly. Whiteboards allow both sides as a team to easily create something together in real-time!

If you're on the phone, of course it's more challenging – but conceptually again set the stage and boundaries of the call, and help the client create a compelling and achievable vision with you that pulls them forward.

Killer Salespeople Uncover True Problems Behind Desired Solutions

When asking prospects about their challenges, their pain, they will usually in fact actually tell you their desired solutions, which sound like problems: "We need a new marketing system," or, "Our marketing system is dysfunctional," is not a true problem, it's a solution masked as a problem. What they are really saying is, "We want a new marketing system."

This isn't because they are hedging – often they just haven't thought about the root source of their problems. In other words, prospects usually don't know what their underlying problems are, and you must help them determine what they are.

Here is a sample of how asking "Why?" or, "Why is that important?" or, "So what?" can lead you to the true business problem:

- "We need to integrate our financial and sales systems." That is a desired solution, not a pain or challenge... Why?

- "Because our reporting is inaccurate." Still not a root challenge yet... Why?

- "Because our executive has presented reports to the CFO that later turned out to be wrong."

Aha! Now that is a real pain: unable to make effective plans or business decisions because of inaccurate reporting.

The challenge of determining these true problems is tough for sales reps who aren't practiced at it. Do regular role-playing in your sales teams to improve the team's skills, and play devil's advocate. Give them lots of solutions that sound like problems, and challenge them to dig the true problems out of you.

Prospects Should Earn Proposals

Does your sales team give out proposals and quotes like one of those people standing on the street handing out flyers? "Here, please take one!"

There is a cost to giving out proposals or paperwork too soon – the prospect doesn't value it or your time, and you lose the chance to set up a specific next step that would help them earn the proposal.

Example:

- You do a demo.
- At the end of the demo, they ask about pricing or a proposal.
- You say you'll include a proposal with a follow up email.
- They say, "Thanks."
- You send the materials.
- You never hear from them again.

Giving out proposals too easily helps no one – though it might feel good to think, "Sent out another proposal today!" Great – but how many are you getting back?

If you're not winning at least 50% of the proposals you're giving out, you're too easy.

Instead, next time when the prospect casually asks about pricing or getting a proposal, don't give it to them until you know they want it. Tell them you'd be happy to, and to do that, you'd need to set up a scoping call with them and the key people, to ensure the proposal is accurate and meets their needs.

If the prospect declines – then either they aren't a great prospect, or you didn't prove your value to them in your prior calls or demos.

If the prospect wants what you have, now you have another chance to focus your time with them and the other key people on creating a vision of how you can specifically solve their problems... and generate a proposal that nails it for them.

If this scares you at first, just try it. You'll see the balance of power shift from being totally uneven and in their favor, to being more of a mutual balance.

My Favorite Sales Call Question Of All Time

I've always been irritated by meaningless questions like "How are you doing today?" I mean, does the person asking actually care or not? And getting called can feel like a violation, even when it's someone you know.

This tip is a small but critical detail, which is why it deserves its own section. In fact, Steel Shaw, who worked for me at Salesforce.com, often said later that this question was the best sales tip he'd ever learned.

Without further adieu, this is the best question ever to use to open calls:

"Did I catch you at a bad time?"

Conversationally, it might be used like this to open a call: "Hi ____, it's Aaron from PebbleStorm calling. Hey by the way, did I catch you at a bad time?"

While this question is useful for any call, it is most useful with unscheduled calls, when the person isn't expecting you (even if they know you).

It helps you make a positive first impression and set the tone of the first two minutes of the conversation, which then determines the rest of the call (and even whether you get to have the call at all).

When you begin a call with "Did I catch you at a bad time?" you're asking permission to chat and putting them at ease; they feel less defensive or violated.

It's much better than "Is this a good time?" (No – it's never a good time for busy people).

Here's what will usually happen when you use this question – they'll say something like either:

- "No, what's going on?"
- "Yes, but I have a minute, how can I help you?"

If they pick up the phone, and it truly is a bad time for them, they'll say so, and you have the perfect opportunity to ask, "When would be a better time to talk? Do you have your calendar handy?"

Though I'm not a pushy or controlling person, **MAKE YOUR TEAM USE THIS QUESTION RELIGIOUSLY!**

6

Lead Generation and "Seeds, Nets & Spears"

Why do people treat all leads alike? They aren't created equal! You need to understand the different types of leads in order to lay a solid foundation for a predictable sales machine.

Distinguishing Leads: "Seeds, Nets and Spears"

I've seen incredible confusion and misunderstanding — among CEOs, Marketing VPs, board members and Sales VPs — around "leads." The parties lack a shared understanding around lead types and how to make rational projections, creating miscommunication, conflict and disagreements.

The most common mistake is lumping all the types of leads into one bucket of "leads," and then making future projections based on past results.

After hearing time and time again about these frustrations, I came up with simple distinctions between the three fundamentally different kinds of leads: "Seeds," "Nets" and "Spears."

However, different leads have different fundamental attributes: how well they qualify, how fast they close, ROI, etc.

I find that thinking in terms of Seeds, Nets and Spears gives teams a simpler way to come to a common understanding (and to share this understanding with investors) of their leads analysis and projections.

Seeds take a lot of time to cultivate and to ramp up, but once they get going, they are unbeatable with the highest conversion and close rates. These include developing happy customers, organic internet search/SEO, public relations, local user groups, most social media, publishing expert content.

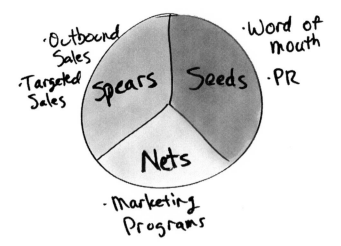

Nets: Nets are classic marketing programs, in which you're trying to cast a wide net and see what you get, whether through email marketing, conferences, advertising, and some forms of internet marketing (PPC).

Spears involve targeted outbound efforts (such your classic "hunting") that require some individual human efforts (such as business development, "Top 10 Targets" programs, and Cold Calling 2.0).

Example "Nets" Marketing Funnel

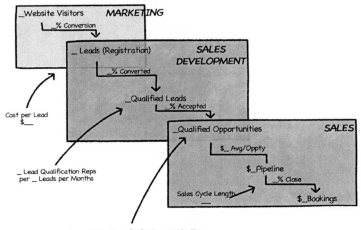

Example "Spears" Prospecting Funnel

Example Cold Calling 2.0 Funnel

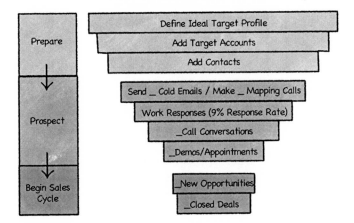

Defining Prospects, Leads, Opportunities, Clients and Champions

Here are my definitions. What is more important than how you define a Lead or any other term, is that everyone has a shared understanding of that definition.

Prospects (or Names)

A database of names or a list that you are marketing to, in which people have not responded positively yet.

If you buy a list of names from a place like InfoUSA, Jigsaw or Hoovers, it is a list of prospects (or names), not "leads."

Leads

A lead is a prospect that has responded positively in some way to show their interest in what you have to offer, such as registering for a white paper or attending a webinar. Whether or not they are a high-quality lead isn't the point – if they've registered for something, they are a lead.

Opportunities

After someone has qualified a lead through email or the phone, and the lead meets your set of qualification criteria, it becomes an opportunity. A common abbreviation is "oppty."

Clients

They have given you money.

Champions

A champion can be a client or non-client that has referred you business, offered a testimonial, or has actively supported you in any other way.

Be sure to give them love!

Use "Layers Of The Onion" To Sell For You

More than ever, prospects like to get to know you first before they buy, and they want to do it on their own terms, and in their own time.

Spend any time with me talking about lead generation or sales, and the term "layers of the onion" or "onion layers" will come up—a lot. I've found that this concept is a great analogy to help teams think through laying out their products and offers.

The goal is to make it easier for prospects to "choose their own adventure" in how they get to know a company and its products, step-by-step.

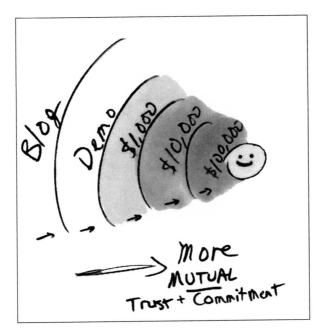

The Internet has drastically shifted power from sellers to buyers. The old way of marketing and selling involved pushing information onto prospects and then working to control their steps along a sales process.

Buyers had limited access to information, which they had to negotiate out of sellers. Now, buyers can do more research on their own before they ever talk to a human at a company (if they ever do talk to a human!)

Go With It – Let Prospects Do The Work!

Instead of resisting this trend and staying attached to how potential customers used to or "should" get to know your company, go with it and give the prospects the control over how they want to get to know you.

Present them with a couple of logical next steps and let them decide how and when to move forward (of course, with some helpful reminders now and then if they've stalled).

Setting up progressive layers of the onion is key to "receiving sales" or "pulling sales" (much easier than pushing sales). Let the prospects do the work for you!

The Layers Are Mutual – Get To Know The Prospects As They Get To Know You

The layers enable prospects and vendors to test mutual compatibility with progressive steps of increasing trust and commitment, to minimize risk and costs of a bad fit to both parties. With the layers of the onion, a prospect can engage right away at the level they feel comfortable with, and then can work their way up the trust and commitment layers as they and you see fit.

As a seller, now you can more easily test out how much of a fit the customer is for you, before you commit extra time or resources to them! Committing to a bad-fit customer is an enormous cost, and the right layers can help you avoid those landmines.

Let Go

Give up trying to control how long someone takes to move forward. You'll have to accept that most prospects who initially sign up for a blog, trial or demo just won't be ready to do anything. That's okay – don't try to force them. But consider if there's another onion layer you can create to offer to make it easier for them to take another step.

Give up trying to control how long someone takes to move forward.

If you see prospects getting stuck somewhere in your "layers," consider redesigning your next-step offers. What is the next "juicy morsel" they would want if

110

you showed it to them, that would help them take another step forward? What new layers, content or products can you create that are compelling and relevant to who the prospect is and where they are in their evaluation and buying cycle?

Let go of trying to control prospects, and trust that if it's a good mutual fit, and you keep nurturing them, and your "layers" are relevant and useful, they will become a customer someday!

How To Generate A Steady Flow Of Inbound Leads

The following section was guest-written by Peter Caputa of Hubspot. When Peter and I first connected, we immediately appreciated each other's thinking, and I'm happy to share some great ideas from Peter on ways to generate inbound leads.

Inbound leads are leads that come to you, typically registering on your website in some way or asking to be called back. They are the ones that find you before you find them.

Inbound leads can be highly erratic, coming in spurts and spikes depending on the winds of fate and what kinds of PR or advertising your company is doing at any one time. But there are ways to create more flow and predictability.

What Inbound Marketing Methods Work?

Each of the activities is ranked in order of its ability to generate leads more easily:

1. Referrals
2. Free Tools/Free Trials
3. Organic Search Engine Optimization
4. Blogging
5. Email Newsletters
6. Webinars
7. PPC (pay-per-click marketing)
8. Affiliate Marketing
9. Social Media

However, all the activities are complementary and can be hard to separate from each other. For example, blogging helps SEO and email newsletters. Collectively, they create an inbound marketing strategy in which each piece complements the others.

Also, pretty much every one of these methods is responsible for doing two important things in inbound marketing.

1. They attract new prospects.
2. They help nurture existing leads.

If I were a marketing or sales VP or a small business owner starting inbound marketing, I wouldn't leave out any of these. But this stuff doesn't happen overnight. Pick three areas first in which to create momentum, before trying to do them all.

Most of these techniques require a time investment instead of a financial investment. Many of these things support each other. So, it's important to do things in the proper order and to prioritize.

Referrals

Your best marketing and source of inbound leads are happy customers. When customers recommend your product or service to a peer, they're establishing that you're credible and trustworthy. The trust implicit in their relationship with the prospect they're referring is transferred to you.

On the web, you can accelerate the pace of referrals by "entering the conversation," setting the precedent for receiving referrals by giving referrals (the law of reciprocity: you get more of what you give) and by generally making yourself available to speak with new people whether there's an immediate, direct connection between their need and your service or not.

Free Tools/Trials

It's hard to remember now, but ten years ago, very few software companies offered free trials. Everyone was worried that competitors would learn too much, and that salespeople would lose a lot of leverage with prospects.

Salesforce.com changed everything as one of the first companies to offer a full 30-day free trial of its service on its website. It became their #1 lead generation and sales tool!

HubSpot's WebsiteGrader.com is a free SEO and website analysis tool that lets anyone analyze the effectiveness of their site and online marketing. Marketo has all kinds of free training and educational resources. Landslide has an online tool that helps organizations design a sales process for free. Practically every software-as-a-service company out there has some kind of free trial. If there's a way to take a part of your service that is useful by itself and make it free, this will generate more leads and become your best sales tool.

Even if you're a company that doesn't sell software, what kind of free trial can you offer? A free consultation? Free online training videos? Samples of your work? Sample product?

Organic Search Engine Optimization (SEO)

This one takes the most patience, but if it is done right, it is simply a byproduct of doing everything else right. SEO requires thorough keyword research and search engine rank monitoring.

If you do this well, blogging, public relations and social media can support your SEO efforts without an expensive SEO consultant, and without a lot of work dedicated "just" to SEO. The name of the game is to pick keywords, optimize pages with those keywords (could be blog posts) and build links.

The effect of SEO on inbound lead generation is cumulative and compounding. In other words, month after month, as long as you keep creating great content and building smart links, the number of leads generated from SEO goes up and up.

Blogging

You must "enter the conversation" (be a part of online discussions) if you're going to do inbound marketing. There are so many people who start a blog and think it's just about saying smart things or about writing. It's not. It's about having a 2-way conversation. Any good salesperson knows that an effective prospecting call requires the prospect to be talking more than the salesperson.

It's the same way with a blog. It's imperative to be a resource for people and to pro-actively network with your blog by reading other blogs, linking to other blogs and leaving comments on other blogs, if you want people to do the same thing for you. It's not necessarily the law of reciprocity, but it's the law of participation. Set a simple goal, such as meeting one new blogger per week.

At some point in the lifetime of a blog, after a critical mass of audience is built, things begin to pick up on their own. This can take months or, more likely if you're new, years. Subscribers come out of nowhere, links come from nowhere, random people repost or forward on your blog posts and send a flood of traffic. After a while, you can just focus on creating great content and hosting a great conversation on your blog.

Email And Lead Nurturing

Permission-based direct email marketing is still THE most important marketing technique both to develop new leads and nurture old ones. Email marketing is important to establish your expertise, build relationships and trust with your audience, promote your webinars or live events, and promote your products.

At a minimum, all you need your email system to do is share your blog posts via email and to invite people to events or webinars you're holding.

Are people even visiting your blog? How many people remember to check your blog anyway without a reminder? Make it easy on them and drop it in their inbox. As a rule of thumb, send out an email at least once per month, and no more than 2x per week.

Webinars

Webinars are a great lead nurturing practice. Webinars get them coming back and interacting and learning from you, and offer an easy and compelling reason to spread the word to their friends about what you're doing.

Webinars are a great lead nurturing practice.

80% of webinars are not for selling but for teaching: TEACH people something useful in the webinar. How can you help them do their jobs better?

Webinars establish credibility and communicate what you do in an educational and neutral setting. Webinars are especially valuable as part of a series, where people know to keep looking for the next piece of your story and can tell their friends about it, too.

Make webinars "bigger than you" – make them about the attendees, not your company. An ideal format: hold webinars in which customers are the presenters, and they are sharing with your audience lessons learned in your area of expertise. Some of these lessons are related to your product, and some lessons are not.

"Pay Per Click" (PPC) Marketing

Pay Per Click Advertising can be a very effective lead generation tool. Some business-to-business companies with simple products or services use PPC as their sole or primary online marketing activity.

However, companies selling sophisticated products and services tend to have mixed results with PPC. The more trust-building and education your prospects need, the less likely PPC leads will convert into customers.

Studies conducted have shown that less-educated people tend to click on pay-per-click ads, while more-educated people click on organic search results.

While PPC sometimes can be a source of leads-on-demand, be careful to track their quality in terms of conversion rates to qualified opportunities and to closed deals.

If you're selling to more sophisticated buyers, you'll be better served with focusing on SEO and blogging as your primary activities, and using PPC in experimental ways as you figure out the best online marketing mix.

Affiliate Marketing / Joint Ventures

If you're at a phase of maturity in your marketing where you know who your ideal prospects are, you can identify publications (i.e. forums, blogs, trade magazines, email lists, vertical search engines) that have relevant audiences of those types of prospects.

The best partners are bloggers or companies with large and trusting email audiences, and whose interests and values align with yours. Better than buying lists from them is placing a compelling offer on a targeted site or in their email newsletter.

Even more ideal: you can partner with them on a (disclosed) pay-for-performance basis, in which they help promote your company in exchange for a pay-per-lead or percentage-of-revenue basis.

Both partners win this way: the blogger/organization creates value for their audience and earns extra income or revenue, and the company generates leads or sells product.

Social Media

Online networking, social media and social bookmarking sites are great tools to support blog readership growth and to support search engine rankings. But I've found that the ROI from social media isn't cumulative or compounding when used in isolation - unless you're already famous.

I do think it's a very important part of an inbound marketing mix as it adds a human face to your company. However, it does not immediately drive a lot of direct traffic that converts into leads.

Social media can also be extremely powerful if a sales and marketing team coordinates some social media marketing activities and leverages the distributed team's personal networks to launch a product, get feedback and raise awareness about a campaign. Sites like LinkedIn and Twitter also make it a bit easier to initially connect with a prospect or lead who seems immune to voicemails and emails.

Do Fewer Things, Better

Do not try to do everything at once! Pick two or three of the above options to begin with and focus on first, building some expertise, momentum and results, before beginning to add more activities. Beware of scattering your energy in too many directions and projects at any one time.

Marketing Automation Best Practices: "How Marketo Uses Marketo"

When you want to learn how to do something really well, where do you go? To the master!

When I wanted to learn how to build the best sales organization possible, I knew where to go: working in sales at Salesforce.com. While I was there, I saw first hand how effective the sales organization became, in large part because Salesforce.com was an expert at developing and using its own product to push the boundaries of sales best practices.

For this book, as a complement to the sales best practices, I wanted to share some modern marketing automation best practices. For that, where better to go than to the marketing department of a hot marketing automation company, Marketo? They've grown from nothing to more than 500 customers in just a handful of years.

Marketo's marketing automation solution, "Marketo Lead Management", helps marketers automate and measure demand generation campaigns. They tie together a variety of functions like email marketing, lead nurturing and lead scoring.

Generating leads is half the battle. To help sales make the most of leads, Marketo's second product ("Sales Insight") helps salespeople understand, prioritize and interact with the hottest leads and opportunities.

I wanted to know how Marketo uses their own Marketo product, because they're experts at using their own product to push marketing automation best practices.

In 2007, when I was at Alloy Ventures, I met Phil Fernandez (CEO) and Jon Miller (VP Marketing) of Marketo. Since then, I've been impressed at their marketing execution and expertise. I believe in what they're doing, and Marketo has also become a partner, client and sponsor of my "Predictable Revenue" work, including this book.

They were generous enough to share some step-by-step inside secrets on what works for them.

118

How Marketo Efficiently Nurtures, Scores And Delivers Tons Of Qualified Leads To Sales

Let's begin with…

The Big Picture: Marketo's "Revenue Funnel"

Marketo's revenue funnel is a visualization of how a prospect typically moves through a buying cycle. They've mapped out at a high level the stages at which prospects go from "nothing" to "customer."

Marketo's funnel has six stages: Awareness, Inquiry, Prospect, Lead, Opportunity and, ultimately, Customer. This book addresses the first four stages, "Awareness" through "Lead."

Throughout the entire process, Marketo uses its product to track the behaviors and actions of its prospects. Here's Marketo's funnel diagram:

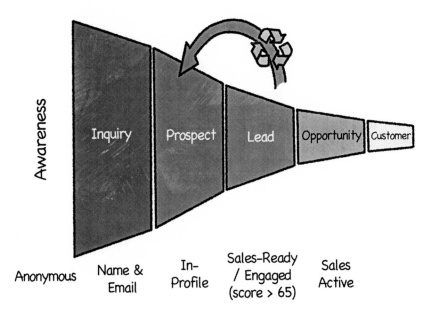

Let's walk through their marketing steps (Awareness, Inquiry, Prospect, and Lead) one-by-one.

Stage 1. "Awareness"

Awareness is when the prospect first discovers the company. At this point in the first four stages, the lead is typically anonymous – that is, Marketo doesn't know their name or any contact information. And yet Marketo still tracks activity levels at this stage.

For example:

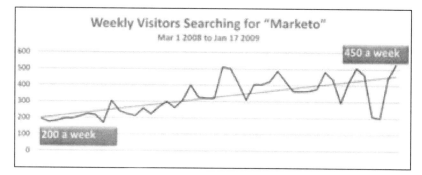

The primary way Marketo tracks "Awareness Activity" levels is by a) observing the number of known or anonymous leads that are visiting the site, or b) searching for the keyword, "Marketo."

Marketo believes that their "Modern B2B Marketing" blog (http://blog. marketo.com) is the main reason the market's awareness of them grew so quickly and greatly sped up how fast they landed their first 500 customers.

This is a really important lesson about blogging and marketing: Marketo doesn't "pitch" their own products on the blog. There's no selling. Marketo's blog is popular and successful because they provide a platform to share all kinds of modern marketing best practices and thought leadership. They invite all kinds of other thought leaders to share on their blog (I've been a guest writer). They've become a trusted authority.

Creating a company blog is a great way to establish brand presence, drive SEO rankings and give prospects and partners an easy way to get to know and trust your company. It is a place to prove your company as a thought leader in your vertical or industry.

Your blog is not the best place to directly promote your business or service. When people get real value from your blog (and events, newsletter and webinars), they will both come back to buy and refer friends.

Stage 2. "Inquiry"

This is the stage when an anonymous lead becomes known by registering with a name and an email address (that's it!) They've now signed up to receive updates from Marketo.

Most of Marketo's website content is open and free to read without having to register. Only certain premium content and research papers require a prospect to fill out a registration form. People hesitate to register even for free content when they first find you, before they get to know you even a little bit.

Even when they begin asking for someone's information, Marketo has a neat capability of "progressive profiling": instead of asking someone to fill out a big long form (reducing conversion rates), Marketo can ask for information bit by bit as someone registers for different pieces of content.

This makes it easier for a prospect to trust the company in small steps while the company continues to learn more about the prospect.

The first time a prospect registers, they might be asked to share only their name and email address. The next time the prospect downloads a new piece of content, the forms are pre-filled and can ask for additional information such as title and company.

Stage 3. "Prospect"

Now we're getting into an area where language is critical. The definitions of "Prospect" vs. "Lead" are especially important to prevent confusion across sales and marketing.

Marketo differentiates "prospects" (colder) from "leads" (warmer). Why: it is highly inefficient to evenly spread sales' time across all leads. Marketo wants to prioritize where its sales team spends its time on lead follow up.

They tell them apart by the "lead score," which rates how hot or not someone is, on a scale of 1 to 100.

Potential buyers with fewer than 65 points are called "prospects"; potential buyers with more than 65 points are called "leads" – the higher the number of points, the hotter the lead. To wrap up this section on "Prospects", let's get into the lead scoring details.

How Marketo Uses Lead Scoring To Prioritize Leads

The system is simple: the more points a lead has (on a scale of 1-100), the hotter the lead.

Leads get points added or subtracted based on aspects like how recently a lead visited and how frequently they visit. Marketo also takes into consideration other factors, such as keywords, content subject matter and actions that should increase or diminish scores, i.e., visiting the career page.

Marketo also implements "score decay." This involves decreasing a lead's score if they become inactive and get colder and colder and colder.

Demographics
- 30 points based on manual Prospect review
- 0-8 points based on title

Source and Offer
- Website leads source: +7
- Thought leadership offer: -5

Behavioral Engagement:
- Visit any webpage or open any email: +1
- Watch demos: +5 each
- Register for webinar: +5
- Attend webinar: +5
- Download thought leadership: +5
- Download Marketo reviews: +12
- More than 8 pages in one visit: +7
- Visit website 2x in one week: +8
- Search for "Marketo": +15
- Visit pricing pages: +5
- Visit careers pages: -10 (I especially love this one!)

No Activity in One Month:
- Score >30: -15 points
- Score 0 to 30: -5 points

If you want to implement this kind of service, don't worry about getting this perfect or as detailed as Marketo! Marketo created its own lead scoring process and points system over time with a lot of experimentation, and they keep evolving it.

The important thing is to get started, look at the results, learn and evolve your scoring processes until they begin to be useful.

Stage 4. "Lead"

Let's say a prospect scores above 65 points, and now officially becomes a "lead." Now what?

Once a prospect becomes a lead, it means that they are someone who is truly interested in Marketo – the company, product or service.

At this point, the sales team knows it is definitely worth their time to follow up on the lead to qualify it and move it into a sales cycle.

Sample Lead Conversion Rates

One of the five critical metrics you must track is lead conversion. What percentage of new leads turn into qualified opportunities?

Here's some example data on Marketo's conversion rates:

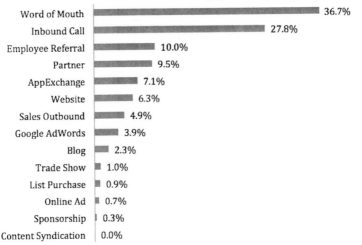

Conversion: Raw Lead to Opportunity

Word of Mouth	36.7%
Inbound Call	27.8%
Employee Referral	10.0%
Partner	9.5%
AppExchange	7.1%
Website	6.3%
Sales Outbound	4.9%
Google AdWords	3.9%
Blog	2.3%
Trade Show	1.0%
List Purchase	0.9%
Online Ad	0.7%
Sponsorship	0.3%
Content Syndication	0.0%

Keeping In Touch With Automated Lead Nurturing Campaigns

Marketo touches buyers in their revenue funnel with four main types of automated lead nurturing campaigns:

1. New Prospect and Lead Campaigns

When a prospective buyer registers on the site for content, such as for a demo or a free trial, it kicks off a series of automatic follow up emails.

For example, 11 minutes after the content is viewed or downloaded, a targeted email is automatically sent from the "Lead Owner" to the prospect. The Lead Owner is the Market Response Rep (or "rep") automatically assigned by the system to own the lead. So automatically every single lead receives an email from their assigned rep. The rep doesn't have to remember to check their new leads every hour. Prospects get FAST follow up from Marketo.

Then, the Market Response Rep manually reviews new leads to determine which ones look like viable prospects, and which ones are junk, spam or other kinds of wastes of time.

After the decision is made that a visitor is a viable prospect, Marketo begins their 21-day follow up campaign:

21-Day Follow-Up Campaign

> Day 1: Evaluation: Over 65 points?
>
> Day 2: Make Phone Call and Send First Email
>
> Day 5: Content Offer Email (invitation to receive more content)
>
> Day 9: Phone Call
>
> Day 16: Email
>
> Day 21: "Recycle"

If the prospect does not engage actively, they then receive "Stay In Touch Campaigns."

2. "Stay in Touch" Campaigns

These campaigns build relationships with leads needing time to "ripen," who aren't yet ready to actively engage with sales.

Also known as a "drip campaign," Marketo sends relevant and useful small pieces of content to leads over time. This builds trust with leads, helps them move along in their buying cycle, and reminds leads to contact Marketo first when the buying cycle becomes active.

Nurturing leads isn't just about making lots of touches — quality is more important than quantity.

Marketo's Five Tips for Effective Lead Nurturing:

- *Make it valuable to them, not just you*
- *Make it bite-sized*
- *Match your content to buyer profiles*
- *Match your content to buying stages*
- *Get the timing right*

The Marketo Lead Lifecycle

If a prospect exceeds 65 points, they are officially called a "lead" and their status is changed to "Lead" in Marketo and salesforce.com systems.

After this status change occurs, Marketo starts an automated 21-Day lead lifecycle process.

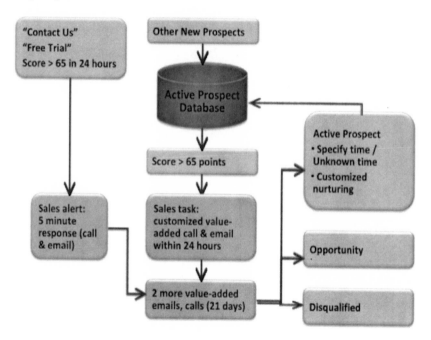

(I know it's hard to believe, but this diagram came from Marketo, not me.)

This process has multiple tracks and three outcomes. The tracks include:

Fast Track: If a lead fills out a "contact me" form, requests a free trial or achieves a score of 65+, these leads receive personal follow-up within five minutes of their activity. The Inside Sales Reps get an automated and instant alert, telling them to follow-up with this lead immediately either by phone or email.

Other New Prospects: If a prospect reaches a lead scoring threshold of 65 points but doesn't match the "fast track" behavior, a sales task is set for the sales rep telling them to interact with this prospect within 24 hours.

In those 24 hours, the inside sales rep researches the company and to get a sense of who they are, their business model and what their marketing needs might be. From there, the sales rep crafts a customized introduction and reaches out to the prospect, and is better prepared to have a productive conversation when they connect with the lead by phone or email.

Marketo's Qualification Criteria

Here are Marketo's five primary criteria:

1. Is there a Compelling Event?
2. Has a Clear Key Pain or Need been Identified?
3. What are the Current Marketing Tools and Processes?
4. What is the Timeframe?
5. What is the Annual Revenue/Size of Company?

If a prospect cannot be reached by phone, Marketo sends two emails and one more call.

After the 21-day process there are three possible outcomes. A lead is either:

1. Disqualified: A small fraction of leads that will never be a good fit.
2. Converted to Opportunity: Inside Sales rep hands off lead to a Account Executive. If this lead is something the Market Response Rep deems pursuable, they convert it into an opportunity.
3. Recycled: These leads receive ongoing nurturing through email marketing. Sales reps can either go back or take the initiative to reach out to these past leads, or reps can wait until a lead takes a new action and is flagged as an active lead.

Make It Ridiculously Simple For Sales Reps To Prioritize

Marketo uses Salesforce.com for their sales force automation system. In addition, Marketo enhances their use of Salesforce.com with their own add-on product, Sales Insight. This application makes it easy for sales reps using Salesforce.com to quickly spot and stay focused on their hottest prospects.

The dashboard provides a visual of the relevant fit and demographics of the lead (stars) and the urgency in which the lead needs to be followed up on (flames):

With one view, the sales rep can see all the accounts in their territory with activity, drill down easily, and then prioritize with whom to spend their time.

How To Find Out More

Whether you are actually interested in Marketo's products or not, you can also learn a lot just by researching their site and registering, then watch how they follow up with you:

www.Marketo.com

Maximize Your ROI From Tradeshows and Conferences

This section is not meant to replace whatever you're doing currently with conferences – it is to give you an additional way to generate leads from them by using your sales team.

Conferences and tradeshows have a bad (ok, terrible) reputation for generating worthwhile leads - for good reason! Most tradeshow attendees are overwhelmed with the amount of activity and options at a show. They are bombarded with free giveaways to get them to give their names up. They sign up for everything for freebies, regardless of whether they care about the product or not.

It's not the fault of tradeshows – the responsibility for lead generation falls to the attendees, who have to carefully think through the whole lead generation process (including prior preparation and post-event follow through) on how to generate real business from the event.

You need a process that emphasizes quality of leads over quantity of names.

The Event Team

Who is the person responsible for lead generation for this specific event?

Who is the "event sales team"? (Who are the sales reps/people doing the work?) It's best to have a consistent team of people for the entire process: preparation, execution at the event, and follow through.

How is success going to be measured? This is never about the number of names logged at an event. Is it the numbers of leads qualified within 2-4 weeks? Is it qualified pipeline generated after 1-3 months? Closed business over the next 2-6 months?

Phase 1: Preparation

Research as much as you can to shape a list of who and which companies are attending. Preferably do this at least 3-4 weeks in advance, because you will need more lead time than you think.

Review and really prioritize the list. Go for quality over quantity: it's better to target fewer, better-fit companies.

Have the event sales team prospect in and make initial contact to research the targets: Do they have a current competitive system? Who are the right decision makers to target?

They might even be able to set up some appointments for the actual event.

Prepare a "Cheat Sheet" summarizing key points about the target companies at the event. This information makes it easy to start real conversations with target prospects ("I understand from John Davis that you use Siebel in your Institutional division....").

Phase 2: Execution At The Event

Have members of the sales team staff the event, and give them time to proactively go out and find the target prospects to approach (cheat sheet in hand of course).

Log every conversation as soon as possible in Salesforce.com, to ensure the details don't get lost in the shuffle.

DISQUALIFY people and avoid indiscriminately scanning every badge that comes by your booth! If you can actually determine if some people would be a waste of time as a prospect, it's better to reduce the clutter and keep them out of the leads list! There is a real cost to keeping low-quality leads on sales reps call list: 1) it makes it harder to find and focus on the good leads, and 2) sales reps will be wasting their time calling on low-quality leads.

Phase 3: Follow Through

Have that same Event Sales Team continue to prioritize and work the list of target prospects, which should now be that much further along the prospecting cycle because of all the contact made at the event.

What can you do to make the next tradeshow even more successful? What worked or didn't?

7

Seven Fatal Sales Mistakes CEOs and Sales VPs Make

I never make stupid mistakes. Only very, very clever ones.
John Peel

Even Experienced CEOs And Sales VPs Make These Mistakes All The Time

I've consulted with dozens of companies since leaving Salesforce.com. Time and time again, I've seen executives repeat the same, fundamental mistakes as they work to grow sales.

Fatal Mistake 1: Not Taking Responsibility For Understanding Sales and Lead Generation

Everything begins with the CEO. Even when a CEO hires executives to run lead generation and sales, the CEO cannot delegate their own understanding of how lead generation and sales works. The CEO must understand the fundamentals in order to set effective goals, coach executives, and solve revenue problems.

One of my own fatal mistakes as the CEO of LeaseExchange was my delegation of both the execution and my understanding of lead generation and sales to others. Not only did I help create arbitrary revenue goals, but I also failed to really understand the "why" when results didn't come in as expected... which means that I didn't have a clear idea of what needed to change in order to get the desired results.

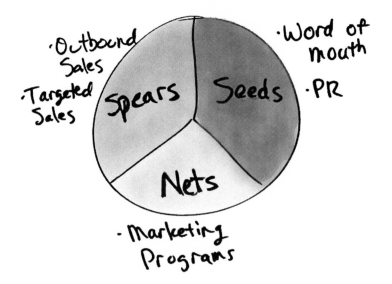

By having an understanding of how sales and lead generation works, your CEO can help create realistic plans and visions for the team. The CEO can avoid arbitrary goals, assumptions, and plans, and thus run a much faster growing, profitable company.

Solution: The CEO takes full responsibility for educating themselves, whether indirectly through coaching, or directly by getting involved in actual projects.

Fatal Mistake 2: Thinking Account Executives Should Prospect (Making Account Executives Jacks-Of-All Trades)

Your need your Account Executives (quota-carrying salespeople) to spend most of their time fulfilling deals or calling on customers, and a minimum of time prospecting for brand new accounts. Prospecting doesn't bring in revenue – closing brings in revenue.

The bulk of prospecting into new accounts should be owned by a separate, dedicated prospecting role.

Account Executives should prospect for new clients less than 20% of the time, and only to a Top 10 Strategic Accounts list, with partners, or to current customers.

The bulk of prospecting into new accounts should be owned by a separate, dedicated prospecting role. Even for businesses such as consulting that depend highly on relationships, much of the early work of new account research, development, and qualification can be handled by cost-effective, focused Sales Development Reps.

Solution: Specialize sales roles. You only need two salespeople to begin specializing. This is so important that I discuss this in multiple places in the book.

Fatal Mistake 3: Assuming Channels Will Do The Selling For You

A giant mistake is assuming that even if you can sign up some channel partners, they will do most of the selling for you.

Usually (especially in software and business service), they won't. Or can't. Or they just aren't very good at it.

You have to control your own destiny. You have to build your own sales results first, and prove your success, before you'll be able to benefit much from channel partners.

The channels will come AFTER you are successful.

Solution: First control your own destiny by building direct sales success before counting channel chickens.

Fatal Mistake 4: Talent Fumbles (Hiring, Training, Incenting)

Predictable Revenue requires you have repeatable people processes. For example, "sink or swim training" in which new hires have to fend for themselves after a few hours or couple of days of training is not repeatable.

Executives make all kinds of other mistakes here, including:

- **Hiring Poorly:** Especially in sales leadership (i.e., taking the resume at face value). Remember, salespeople are talented at SELLING–including themselves!
- **Insufficient Training:** Back to training... new hires should spend time in any services area that works with live customers before starting their "real" job, to learn what it's like to be in the customer's shoes. See the graphic below for an example of the "ladder training" approach.

Train New Employees in Support / Services
Very important: train salespeople in non-sales roles

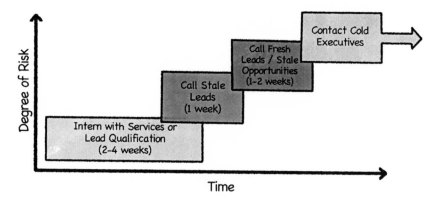

- **Misguided Ramp Time Expectations**
  - Think 1-3 months for inside Account Executives, and up to 6-18 (yes 18!) months for field or enterprise Account Executives.
  - What is the best way to help them ramp faster? Help them with lead generation, rather than counting on them to develop 100% of their own deals.
- **Promoting the Wrong People**: Why don't executives ask "the people" for their input on who should be promoted?
- **Using Money as the Main (or only) Motivator**: And ignoring softer but more powerful forms of rewards such as respect, appreciation, and fun.

Solution: Stop reinventing (and breaking and reinventing...) the wheel on your own. Get coaching on how to hire, train, and incent, or find local companies to model.

Fatal Mistake 5: Thinking "Product-Out," Not "Customer-In"

If your sales or lead generation efforts are struggling, first look to yourself. How clear is your Ideal Customer Profile? Have you identified their core challenges? Are you marketing to and speaking to those ideal clients, or are you speaking to too broad an audience, and diluting your voice?

Executives hate to do this because they feel like they are shrinking their market opportunity, but the wisdom says, "Pick a niche, get rich." Think of a fire hose: If it's on a wide spray, it doesn't go far. But tighten it to a laser-thin stream, and it will punch through a wall. Think of your messaging the same way. Is it tight enough to punch through a market's noise and indifference? It's the same amount of water and energy, just with a different focus.

Also, companies love to talk about what they do and what they are. "We are the leading platform in ..." No one cares about what you do; they only care what you can deliver for them. You're a "platform"? Why is that valuable to customers? What is the impact or result you can promise customers?

Executives need to spend at least 25% of their time with customers, so they stay connected with "what it's really like out there."

Solution: Talk to customers to get clear on what you do for them, rather than how you do it. Put this into a simple, clear one-page document you can share with the entire company. Regularly connect with customers by phone or in person.

Fatal Mistake 6: Sloppy Tracking And Measurement

You can't have predictability without having repeatable processes. You can't make what counts repeatable if you're not regularly measuring what matters (and that doesn't include the number of dials per day your salespeople make).

- How effectively are you measuring your sales and marketing activities and results?

- If you aren't... why do you keep putting it off? "We'll do that next week, quarter, year..."

- Unless you understand what works and doesn't work, you are only guessing at how to improve.

If You Only Track Five Metrics...

Track as many of these as you can in your sales force automation system's dashboards:

1. New leads created per month (also, from what source).

2. Conversion rate of leads to opportunities.

3. Number of, and pipeline dollar value of, qualified opportunities created per month. This is the most important leading indicator of revenue!

4. Conversion rates of opportunities to closed deals.

5. Booked revenues in three categories: New Business, Add-On Business, Renewal Business.

Solution: Start tracking 3-5 key activities or results now. Keep experimenting with new metrics, old ones, and how you can use them to improve your business. Review them weekly with a core team.

Fatal Mistake 7: Command-And-Control Management

Do you find it easier to tell people what to do, rather than coaching them through it, even though it takes longer and more of your energy and attention?

You aren't alone. It can be challenging to spend a lot of time focused on supporting your people, and it's tempting to think "they're adults, they can figure it out."

The danger is that you end up treating employees like resources, rather than people with lots of potential, energy and ideas they could contribute given the right circumstances.

In Reality…

- Most employees have ideas and want to contribute beyond their roles.
- Most employees want to be inspired and make a difference.
- Most employees want to be helpful, trusting, and communicative.
- For most employees, it's just as exhausting for them as it is for management to be told what to do all the time.

How can you harness the full creativity, inspiration, and output of your employees? There are plenty of proven practices to help you do this:

Solution: Read "The Seven Day Weekend" by Ricardo Semler, visit Worldblue.com to learn more about democratically run companies, or read *CEOFlow: Turn Your Employees Into Mini-CEOs*.

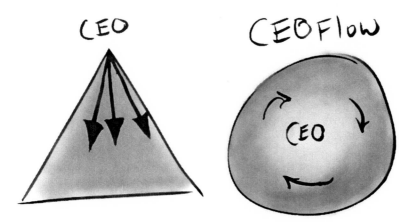

Bonus Mistake: Under-Investing In Customer Success

CEOs and executives, mostly in the early years of a company, are too focused on getting new customers, and frequently ignore current and past ones.

You get one head to hire… should it be a salesperson, or an account management person? Almost always the answer is sales.

Ignore account management and ongoing customer support at your own peril.

We now have a world of "Frictionless Karma." Bad and good customer experiences get around instantly rather than taking a lifetime. One bad apple can spoil a bunch faster than ever.

Hold the hands of your first 50 customers; give them lots of love.

In 2008, I had a client that was in their second pitch meeting with a bank for a potentially enormous deal. They had a coach on the inside, and felt the meeting went great!

A few days after this meeting, their coach contacted them and said, "As a friend, I wanted to let you know that we emailed a bunch of companies we know who use applications such as yours. You are my own personal favorite company, but all the responses we received from your clients said your service is terrible. It's put you behind the 8-ball in this deal." That's not a pleasant message for a VP Sales to receive.

Solution: Hold the hands of your first 50 customers; give them lots of love.

There's no process or magic to this: call them, visit them, talk to them! Ask them what they need, if they have any improvements or ideas to suggest. Ask their advice. Then do something about it.

8

Sales Machine Fundamentals

The basics. And remember, specialize, specialize, specialize!

Happy Customers Create Extraordinary Growth

What do the billion-dollar companies — Salesforce.com, Facebook, Zappos, and Google — all share? Customer trust. Customer success. Customer happiness. Customer delight.

What are you doing to make your customers satisfied, successful and happy?

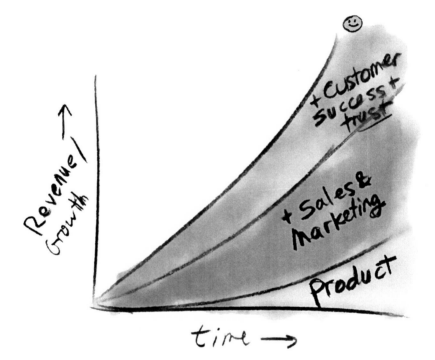

Sales 1.0 (Promotion) And Sales 2.0 (Attraction)

The Internet has changed everything and has caused major shifts in business and sales:

In the past Sales worked in a way that was like someone poking you with their finger, saying, "Going to buy yet?" (Poke) "Going to buy yet?" (Poke) "Going to buy yet?" (Poke)... until you gave in and just bought, even if it was only to get that person off your back.

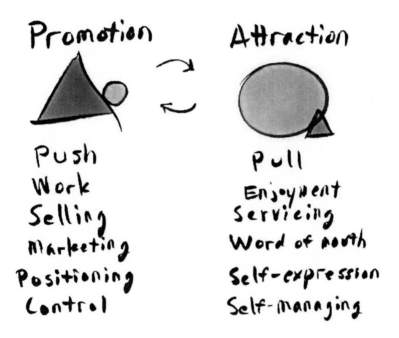

Successful selling also used to be mostly about control and manipulation. It was about getting the deal done and the check-in, without worrying much about what happened afterward. Companies could sell expensive and crappy products and get away with it (at least for awhile). Before the Internet, it was much harder to find out how many customers were unhappy or had been failed.

Now that's all changed, because of the Internet and what I call "Frictionless Karma." (If you do something good or bad, it comes back around to you right away, not in your next lifetime).

Great companies know the sale is just the first step in an ongoing process of making customers successful over a course of years.

Sales in the "Attraction" world we live in now isn't about being passive. You can still be as aggressive as ever—except the tone has changed. Rather than being pushy, all about money, and often coming off as fake, it's about being respectful, purposeful, and adding real value to prospects, even before they become customers. Salespeople should be "pleasantly persistent."

What's Changed?

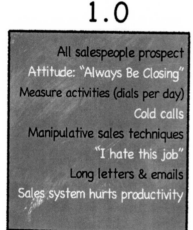

1.0	2.0
All salespeople prospect	Dedicated prospecting team
Attitude: "Always Be Closing"	"Is there a mutual fit?"
Measure activities (dials per day)	Measure results (qualified leads)
Cold calls	Research, referral calls
Manipulative sales techniques	Authentic techniques, integrity
"I hate this job"	"I am learning a valuable skill"
Long letters & emails	Short and sweet emails
Sales system hurts productivity	Sales system helps productivity

Nine Principles Of Building A Sales Machine

While most of this book is about "what" you should do to create predictable revenue through a sales machine, "how" you do it is just as important.

Here are nine fundamentals about how, day-to-day, you can be much more effective in the way you build your sales machine:

1) Be PATIENT. Developing a sales engine that predictably generates revenue can take 4-12 months or more, depending on the state of your company. Even a single new program (such as a lead generation campaign) in business-to-business sales can take months and months to be defined, make your first mistakes, fix 'em, see revenue, and become integrated and habitual.

2) Experiment. With everything. Constantly. A/B test. Try two different phone scripts or emails with 50 prospects, and measure which one works better. And apply this idea to everything you do. Test and see what works.

3) Don't take on one-off projects. (Unless it's an experiment to learn something for the future). If it's not intended to be repeatable, it's not worth doing. One-off efforts, even for a quick payoff, are a distraction from focusing your energy on sustainable efforts.

4) Get out of Excel! Create a rule that if "it" (an opportunity, order, client, etc.) doesn't exist in your sales force automation system, then it doesn't exist. For example, salespeople should only be compensated based on the deals and data that are in your sales system. Reports must be run as much as possible from within Salesforce.com (or whatever your main metric-tracking system is), rather than in Excel.

5) Sketch out how things work and what your processes are on a flow chart. What is your lead generation or sales process? Can you sketch it out simply, on paper or a whiteboard? If not, that's a problem. I am not a fan of complex flow charts – I am easily confused. Even laying out a process in 3-7 high level steps is useful to everyone involved.

Start with defining the desired outcome of a process or team. What does the process have to look like to lead to that outcome? Is this function being done ad hoc today? Sketching it out is the first step to bringing some order to the process... and thus bringing predictability to getting the desired outcome.

6) Focus on results rather than activity. Example: Tracking the number of qualified opportunities created per month is much more meaningful than focusing on the number of sales calls made per day.

7) Track fewer, more important metrics. It's easy to go overboard in over-building reports and dashboards, ending up with "dashboard clutter" in which too many reports and metrics make it difficult to focus on the most important ones. Work with your team to prioritize metrics. Think in handfuls, not dozens.

Five of the most important metrics in lead generation and sales development:

1. **New leads** created per month.

2. **Number of qualified sales opportunities** created per month.

   And the total dollar amount of new qualified pipeline generated this month (the best indicator of future revenue).

3. **Percentage conversion rate** of leads to qualified opportunities.

4. **Total bookings or revenue** (broken out by "New Business," "Add-On Business," or "Renewal Business.")

5. **Win rates.** What percentage of new pipeline resulted in won deals?

8) Pay special attention to "batons" that cross functions. Whenever a process crosses teams (Marketing handing leads to Sales, or Sales passing new clients to professional services, etc.), a "baton" is passed. These hand-offs are the cause of 80% of the problems and defects in your processes. Redesign how the batons are passed to ensure they are passed smoothly and aren't dropped.

9) Take baby steps! Consistently try lots of little improvements. If you keep at them, they'll add up to big changes over time. (Remember the part about patience?) Companies think that they can make bigger changes than they can, faster than is possible... and end up biting off more than they can chew, creating a "two steps forward, two steps back" syndrome.

Separate The Four Core Sales Functions

Building a highly productive, modern sales organization requires increasing specialization—and frankly, it's a big reason Salesforce.com has such an amazingly productive and successful sales organization.

One of the biggest productivity killers is lumping a mix of different responsibilities (such as raw web lead qualification, cold prospecting, closing, and account management) into one general "sales" role.

Inefficiencies Created By "Lumping"

- **Lack of Focus:** Salespeople juggle too many responsibilities, reducing their ability to get things done. Salespeople have a reputation for being ADD – how does adding more responsibilities help that? For example, qualifying web leads is a much lower value distraction for salespeople than managing current clients. And managing a large current client base is a distraction from closing new clients!

- **Harder To Develop Talent:** When you only have one or two sales roles, it's more challenging to bring in raw talent and develop them. There's no progressive step-by-step career path. This is unfortunate, because homegrown talent usually ends up being the best!

- **Unclear Metrics:** It's harder to break out and keep track of key metrics (inbound leads, qualification and conversion rates, customer success rates...) if all the functions are lumped into single areas. Different roles = easier to break out different steps in your processes = better metrics.

- **Less Visibility Into Problems**: When things aren't working, lumped responsibilities obscure what's happening and make it more difficult to isolate and fix issues with accountable follow through.

The Four Core Sales Functions (Or "Themes")

Here are four basic sales functions or themes (I say "themes" because each of these functions can be sub-divided even further as your organization gets bigger):

1. **"Inbound" Lead Qualification:** commonly called Market Response Reps, they qualify marketing leads coming inbound through the website or 800-number. The sources of these leads are marketing programs, search engine marketing, or organic word-of-mouth.

2. **"Outbound" Prospecting/Cold Calling 2.0:** Commonly called Sales Development Reps or new business development reps, this function prospects into lists of target accounts to develop new sales opportunities from cold or inactive accounts. This is a team dedicated to proactive business development.

   Highly efficient outbound reps and teams do NOT close deals, but create and qualify new sales opportunities and then pass them to Account Executives to close.

3. **"Account Executives" or "Sales":** These are quota-carrying reps who close deals. They can be either inside or out in the field. As a best practice, even when a company has an Account Management/Customer Success function, Account Executives should stay in touch with new customers they close past the close until the new customer is deployed and launched.

4. **Account Management/Customer Success:** Client deployment and success, ongoing client management, and renewals. In today's world of "frictionless karma," someone needs to be dedicated to making customers successful – and that is NOT the salesperson!

If you aren't specializing your people into these kinds of roles, this is the very first place to begin! You MUST specialize your people to effectively grow results.

When To Specialize?

I frequently hear, "We're too small to specialize yet." It is always "sooner than you think," even if you just have a handful of Account Executives. The second person you hire, after a salesperson who can close, should be a sales rep who is dedicated just to generating leads for your first closer.

A second rule of thumb is the 80/20 rule. When your reps, as a group, are spending more than 20% of their time on a secondary function, break out that function into a new role.

Specialize Your Four Core Sales Roles

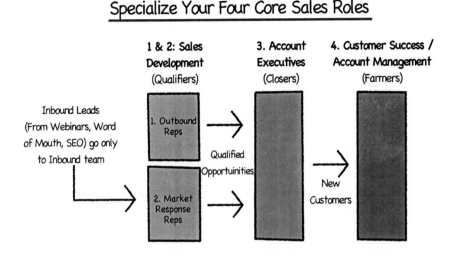

For example, if someone whose primary role is to generate outbound leads begins spending more than 20% of their time qualifying inbound leads, it's time to look at specializing and creating a separate role just for responding to inbound leads.

Likewise, if a field salesperson is spending more than 20% of their time prospecting for new client business (rather than developing business from their current pipeline and customer base), then look at how you can specialize to reduce their prospecting burden.

Regardless of how many Account Executives (AEs) you have, if you're getting a couple of hundred inbound leads per month, you should have an inside Market Response Rep qualifying them for the AEs. If you already have three or four AEs, don't make your next hire another AE. Consider hiring an outbound Sales Development Rep that can spend 100% of their time working to feed the AEs.

Online Presentations

You can find slide presentations on inbound lead management, Cold Calling 2.0, and more on www.PredictableRevenue.com.

If You Sell To Sales Executives...

If you sell to sales executives, change your fiscal year to January 31 or February 28. Why make life unnecessarily harder on yourself by trying to close deals with the very people that are trying to close their own deals at the same time? Salesforce.com, a company that knows something about selling to sales executives, ends their fiscal year January 31st.

Don't expect as many email or phone responses from sales executives as you approach the end of the month or quarter. Be respectful and wait to call them a couple of days after the period ends.

Likewise, most sales executives are on smart phones, so with new prospects, send short emails that are easy to read and respond to, and that don't require a lot of thinking and processing.

If you don't sell to sales executives and this example doesn't apply to you, what can you do to make buying easier? What kinds of patterns or challenges or seasonalities do they live with that you can work around, rather than fight against?

A Totally Different Vision For Structuring Sales Teams

I have a vision for technology companies, one that is already working in some other kinds of services and manufacturing companies.

The management practices of most business-to-business technology and business services industries are in many ways like the manufacturing practices of the giants of old, like General Motors, that were surpassed by the lean giants of late, like Toyota.

I want to see the management and sales models of more companies evolve towards a collection of "businesses inside a bigger business." Rather than being divided into teams based purely on function (Sales, Marketing Services), employees are grouped into mini-business units that include a variety of functional roles in each team.

For example... What if, instead of having massive and distinct teams of people just doing sales, or only doing support, or only marketing, you remixed those employees into mini-business units similar to a retail chain that is composed of lots of mini-businesses (retail stores)?

Say you're a software company. What if you created a "pod-team" mini-business structure with its own territory that included (just as an example) one marketing person, two inside salespeople, two outside salespeople, an account manager, two support people, and a technical expert/sales engineer?

What if each person in that mini-business could learn about customer needs and experiences from each other? Imagine your sales guy, after he's been through basic sales training with other salespeople, is sitting next to a marketing person and a support person...

Wouldn't the salesperson know how to sell more effectively by learning from the marketing and support persons how to speak in the customers' language, avoid problem customers, set expectations, get more referrals and win more deals?

Wouldn't the marketing person learn how to market more effectively by hearing the salesperson sell, and by learning from the support person how customers actually use the product?

149

Wouldn't the support person head off more issues early before they fester, because they've been able to observe the lifecycle of the customer from the point they entered the sales cycle?

What if you measured and compensated the mini-businesses on metrics that completely align with your company's key metrics, such as Revenue, Profitability, and ROI of their mini-business?

What if one of the team was a mini-CEO, who ran the team like a general manager of a retail store or division and managed the financial profit and loss statement of his mini-business: managing hiring, firing, coaching, customer satisfaction and sales?

Can you imagine the kind of talented people you could develop this way, people who could truly be mini-CEOs in your business and help take it to the next level without needing you to hold their hands?

I know someone out there must be doing something like this in technology or other high-value services businesses. I would love to hear from you – reach out and share your system and story and what is working or not working!

9

Cultivating Your Talent

The quality of your people means everything to you and your team's success.

As an old Chinese Proverb says:

If you want one year of prosperity, grow grain.

If you want ten years of prosperity, grow trees.

If you want one hundred years of prosperity, grow people.

Happy Employees Develop Happy Customers

Remember the "Happy Customers Required For Extraordinary Growth" sketch? Well, it begins with developing a great culture in your company first.

What are you doing to help your employees actually enjoy their work? The example you set as a CEO or leader will ripple out (positively or negatively) through the company and culture...

"Where Do I Hire Great Salespeople?"

I'm asked this all the time. Of course it's always hard to find great people, whether in sales or any other function. The best long-term source of salespeople is to grow and develop your own.

Combine one part veteran with three parts young, smart and adaptable... and mix in a system that keeps challenging people to learn new things, to stretch, step by step. The best salespeople are the ones that have grown up in your company, and know it, your products, your customers, inside and out.

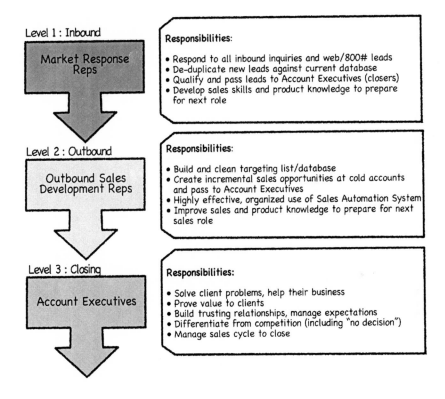

Level 1 : Inbound

Market Response Reps

Responsibilities:
- Respond to all inbound inquiries and web/800# leads
- De-duplicate new leads against current database
- Qualify and pass leads to Account Executives (closers)
- Develop sales skills and product knowledge to prepare for next role

Level 2 : Outbound

Outbound Sales Development Reps

Responsibilities:
- Build and clean targeting list/database
- Create incremental sales opportunities at cold accounts and pass to Account Executives
- Highly effective, organized use of Sales Automation System
- Improve sales and product knowledge to prepare for next sales role

Level 3 : Closing

Account Executives

Responsibilities:
- Solve client problems, help their business
- Prove value to clients
- Build trusting relationships, manage expectations
- Differentiate from competition (including "no decision")
- Manage sales cycle to close

Create A Farm Team System

Think about how you can create a career path for people, to continually develop and grow them. Each group can act as a feeder team to the next. Here's a startup/ small sales team example:

- Market Response Rep (responds to website leads)
- Sales Development Rep (develops new opportunities at cold accounts)
- Account Executive/Sales Executive (closes deals)

You can have a much more specific system with more levels. In the following example, with a larger organization and more roles, each role helps prepare the person to succeed in the next step:

1. Marketing intern or Sales Operations contractor
2. Inside Sales Development – Qualify Inbound Leads
3. Inside Sales Development – Outbound Prospecting
4. Inside Sales Closing – Small/Medium Businesses
5. Inside Sales Closing – Small Field Deals
6. Field Sales Closing – Mid-Market Accounts
7. Field Sales Closing – Enterprise Accounts

And this doesn't even include account management, sales engineers, customer support, and other customer-related teams that always benefit from moving people in and around them.

The more kinds of different experiences your people are exposed to and develop an expertise in, the better equipped they are to become killer problem-solvers for customers! And that's a great thing in ANY role in the company, customer-facing or not.

Timing

Depending on the role, you'll want to move people up the ladder (or rotate into another group) anywhere from 6-8 months on the very fast side, early in the first stages of the system, to 1-3 years in the other stages. Any short-term transaction cost/effort in moving someone into a new role is really outweighed by the benefits of getting a more well-rounded, developed employee who has another learning curve to keep them energized, and a broader understanding of what customers need.

The Very Best Salespeople...

Hire and promote carefully! The best salespeople are more like consultants or business people who can sell than salespeople. In addition, they are the ones who:

- Listen much more than they talk.

- Are problem-solvers.

- Understand their customers' industry/business/needs (key to both building trust with customers as well as understanding how to help solve their problems).

- Believe in their product and company.

- Demonstrate unquestionable integrity.

- Can get things done in their own company (via internal networks).

Are you hiring these kinds of people? Have you written out an "Ideal Employee" profile for your interviewers to help them know who to hire, and how to interview?

How are you training and developing the people you've already hired? If you don't have some kind of training or development program in place, it's probably not happening as much as it should. Even having a one-hour team training session once a week (Tuesday or Wednesday afternoons) can make a big difference in your team's sales skills.

Should You Consider Commission-Only Salespeople?

For 95% of the companies I talk with, I am not a fan of commission-only salespeople. Each executive understands what's best for their unique market and business, but it's hard to imagine a situation in which I would recommend that you hire commission-only salespeople.

The exception is in an industry in which commission-only is a well-known and practiced standard, such as financial services.

Your environment determines whether your people succeed or not, and "commission-only" doesn't demonstrate commitment by the sales leadership or the company that they're really there and incented to help their salespeople succeed.

Pros:

- Reduced risk in hiring (there are still time and opportunity costs).
- Salespeople are highly incented to close business.

Cons:

- If your sales cycles are more than a month or two long, commission-only salespeople will begin starving before they can realistically close enough business. They are more likely to fall out before you can see whether or not they will really work out.

- The company will attract more inexperienced salespeople that can't get better jobs.

- Commission-only increases the motivation to "do wrong" to close a sale. You do not want desperate salespeople representing your company. They will increase your liability, decrease your customer success and satisfaction, and wreck your culture and morale.

- Erratic compensation and lack of reliable income means your salespeople have more financial problems, ironically distracting them from work goals.

If you have a "churn and burn" culture that sells commoditized product, perhaps commission-only sales is a way to go.

If you want to build a solution-selling, high-value sales force, commit the team and company to invest in their success just as much as you expect them to invest in the company!

Internal Training Builds A Better Sales Force

Ongoing training can be the cheapest and easiest (yes, easiest) way to improve your team's performance. It takes commitment and focus, but is always a great investment of your time.

The Best and Cheapest Investment In Your People...

...is consistent, regular training and coaching (especially new hires). I see again and again what a difference regular training makes in improving sales skills and results, reducing ramp time and increasing "promotability" (yeah, I just made that word up, but what a concept!).

Simple monitored practice exercises, with feedback, can make a dramatic, noticeable difference in performance, whether in public speaking, objection handling, phone skills, demos or personal/career development.

What Works

- A program with an ongoing, regular format.
- Includes exercises/role-playing and useful feedback.
- Is designed effectively, to make it worth your reps' time.
- Follow through on everything: maintain the schedule, check progress, keep it fresh and don't let things slip.

Finally, the most important thing to making this work is commitment from the CEO or VP Sales to follow through and stick to it. You will have kinks to work out over weeks, months or quarters. Internal training will only get the attention and time it deserves if the management team believes in it, and is willing to invest in it.

The Importance Of Follow-through

"One hit wonder" programs without follow-through actually detract from performance: 1) any progress isn't lasting, 2) you've wasted the time and resources invested in the one hit wonder, and 3) your team will see that you or the organization aren't really committed to training... so why bother?

For an ongoing lasting benefit to your productivity, you MUST follow through on each aspect of the program and demonstrate management's commitment to it. If you aren't committed, your sales reps won't be committed.

Example: A New Hire Program and Sales Boot Camp

Does your company have any formal initial training for new salespeople and hires? For example, a "Sales Boot Camp" ending with certification exercises in how reps conduct initial sales presentations and demos?

New hires should be initially ranked by performance for sales executives. Over time, salespeople should annually re-certify on product knowledge and competition, two examples of ever-changing areas.

Example: Embedding Training Into Career Paths

Use internal promotion paths for additional opportunities to train people. When a salesperson wants a promotion, put them through a mock sales situation depending on their level of experience. For example, the most junior people can go through a "first call customer pitch" presentation (the first in-person presentation to a prospect company) as their promotion interview.

This both gives the interviewing sales executives a chance to assess potential, and incents salespeople to invest in developing the skills they need to get to the next sales level (public speaking, objection handling, etc.).

The Best Kind Of Sales Training

Nothing beats role-playing as a form of training. Even compared to live "on the phones" training, my favorite thing about role playing is that you can stop and redo a whole or part of a session time and time again, until someone gets it.

You can use role-playing to train people on calls, demos or live presentations.

How To Do It

First, include role-playing in your new hire training, and in your regular team trainings.

Let's use a role-playing call as an example of how to do it.

- A scenario is created and described to the group. Let's say an SDR is going to call on the VP Marketing at a division of General Electric. Or perhaps they are conducting a discovery call with two executives from that division.

- The trainee is selected.

- One or more people are selected to pretend to be the prospect company. (You can have different people in different roles on a single call or demo: CEO, VP Sales, etc).

- Send off the person to be trained, back to their cube or another room.

- Everyone else goes into a conference room. This includes the others on the sales team, so they can listen in.

- The trainee dials into the conference room... and off you go!

The training lead should challenge the trainee, but not make it so hard that they get frustrated and don't learn anything.

You'll find that it is easier than you think to get into the role, especially if you have any good actors. (By the way, don't fail to notice the "creative types"!)

A Self-Managing Weekly "SalesforceU" Training Meeting

Some functions can be designed to be self-managing without a designated leader. My team had a "Salesforce University" meeting every Wednesday afternoon for ongoing education. We modeled it after the Toastmasters public-speaking organization format, and customized it for our specific business needs.

It was self-organizing. Each week someone would volunteer (or would be volunteered, if they were shy and needed a kick in the pants) to manage the next week's agenda and meeting.

The agenda often included a mix of topics in 10-15 minute chunks, such as:

- Product or sales training.

- General business topics (like understanding financial statements or how to manage people).

- Public speaking: Sales reps would present to the whole team for practice and feedback

- "Dealer's Choice" – anything the agenda owner wanted to include just for fun

The Meeting Leader for that week didn't have to create the content for the next meeting; they were just responsible for finding speakers, organizing them, and running the meeting. This was their own opportunity to begin developing mini-CEO skills at a very basic level.

Here is a specific example of a Salesforce University (SalesforceU) agenda:

1. Meeting Leader Opening (1min): Got the meeting started on time. Introduced first speaker. Kept the meeting on track and on time.

2. Sales Skills 1 (10-20min): We usually used this block for public speaking/presentation practice, from simple first-time presentations up to a full sales role-play exercise, including a business scenario, pitch, objection handling, and competition. Before moving on, the Meeting Leader asked the team to share immediate feedback for the speaker.

3. Quick Questions (10-15min): A team member prepared four to five questions that prospects commonly asked, and calls on people to answer them and get their feet put to the fire! The questions required short 1-2 minute answers. After each answer, other teammates quickly shared their feedback and suggestions of better answers.

4. Sales Skills 2 (10-20min): A second bite-sized session to practice public speaking, role-play phone calls, demos, etc.

5. New Best Practice (10min): The topic owner shared one of their own best practices or found a coworker's worth sharing.

6. Industry/Vertical Learning (15min): Each week we selected a vertical for someone to research. They updated the team with information that helps prospect and sell more effectively: terminology, business model fit (or lack thereof), targeted discovery questions, current reference customers, etc. The content owner of this section ended up being the team expert in that area.

7. Meeting Leader Closing (5min): Closed the meeting by:

   - *Asked for feedback on the SalesforceU format – should it change for next week?*

   - *Chose a SalesforceU Lead for the next session.*

   - *Content owners for the next week were determined.*

The new SalesforceU Lead wrote down the updated roles and was responsible for making following week's meeting successful.

Meetings averaged about an hour to an hour-and-a-half, and the meeting leader was responsible for keeping it on time (another great mini-CEO skills practice). Once in awhile we organized special sessions, such as a full-team demo practice exercise.

I had to consciously pull my energy back and resist "managing."

The manager's only participation was, along with everyone else in the room, to share feedback with speakers, and coach the Meeting Leader if necessary. I had to consciously pull my energy back and resist "managing."

The more I put my energy and presence into the meeting, the less space there was for people to share their own energy and ideas.

The SalesforceU Meeting Leader may not have run a meeting before. It was their responsibility to ask for help and advice about how to run a successful session. There was no shortage of expertise all around them, and there was no excuse for not tapping into it.

With the meeting-to-meeting handoff of roles, and a feedback mechanism built in, the meeting became a self-perpetuating engine.

10

Leadership and Management

Nothing so conclusively proves a man's ability to lead others as what he does from day to day to lead himself.

~Thomas J. Watson

6 Responsibilities Of A Manager

A no-nonsense management model:

1. Choose people carefully
2. Set expectations and vision
3. Remove obstacles
4. Inspire your people
5. Work for your people
6. Improve it next time

1. Choose People Carefully

It often makes sense to hire for talent and adaptability than for experience. Over time, the best employees are ones that can adapt to changing circumstances and roles. A fast-learning, hungry hire can make up for a reasonable lack of experience in 6-12 months, and then surpass more-experienced peers.

My best performing salesperson in 2004 had never held a sales role before he joined our team. If you have a great candidate but are concerned about their experience, consider creating a "starter" role in which to test them for 6 months.

2. Set Expectations And Vision

Don't define the role in terms of activities; rather, define it in results as much as possible. If you lay out a too-inflexible process to achieve results, you 1) prevent individuals from being creative in improving the process, and 2) risk that the process won't connect with some individuals, and they'll underperform.

Tell them where on the map they need to get to, give them advice and guidance, but then let them find their way.

3. Remove Obstacles

Managers also have to act like a professional sports commission that sets and enforces rules, defines the playing field, the referee system, etc., and then stands to let the teams play. If the playing field, rules or refereeing isn't clear and fair, games grind to a halt with uncertainty, arguments and confusion.

- Simplicity, clarity = productivity
- Uncertainty, ambiguity = waste

Likewise in sales, if territories, holdouts and rules of engagement, comp plans and sales processes are undecided or confusing, it creates pure "friction": wasted time and effort with zero benefit.

To create a frictionless environment for your salespeople, set up and update (on time) clear territories, comp plans and holdout/transition rules.

4. Inspire Your People

Inspiring is not cheerleading, it's understanding what helps your team and its individuals find their own reasons (not your reasons) to excel and to achieve their full potential (not your potential).

Compensation structure is part of it, but just as important are regular complements on good work, in both private and public. Opportunities for career advancement, the opportunity to learn or achieve particular goals, and many other factors can affect motivation (or lack thereof).

"Pit bull" management personalities can unfortunately be glorified in media (as in Glengarry Glen Ross) and in some aggressive organizations. These managers are terrible for long-term individual and company productivity. The good people who have options will just leave, leaving your company with all the people who can't get other jobs.

Don't be a pushover either. Balance positive encouragement with discipline.

5. Work For Your People

How satisfied would you be in your job if there was no opportunity to learn, grow or be promoted? Does your own manager take the time to help develop you?

Your people want the same things. Take time to proactively understand their individual life/career goals, then work to help them achieve those goals. Help each person find their right fit and path in the company rather than automatically getting them to the next rung on the promotion ladder.

Treat any mistakes as learning and coaching opportunities.

Rather than thinking that they work for you, cultivate a mindset that you work for your people. The more you work for their success, the more they'll work for the team's success and yours.

6. Improve It Next Time

What would you do differently next time with any of the above five steps? Periodically go back over the above five steps. Improve and change as your company grows. What works today can be improved tomorrow.

Retaining Star Employees

Your company's long-term success will always depend on maintaining and developing great people. Are you at risk of losing any star employees? Would you even know if you were at risk, or will you find out when they tell you of a new offer they just accepted?

There's a great way to measure the satisfaction of your key employees. Buckingham and Coffman's book, First, Break All The Rules: What The World's Greatest Managers Do Differently, outlines 12 key measures for employees:

1. Do I know what is expected of me at work?
2. Do I have the materials and equipment I need to do my work right?
3. At work, do I have the opportunity to do what I do best every day?
4. In the last seven days, have I received recognition or praise for good work?
5. Does my supervisor, or someone at work, seem to care about me as a person?
6. Is there someone at work who encourages my development?
7. At work, do my opinions seem to count?
8. Does the mission/purpose of my company make me feel like my work is important?
9. Are my co-workers committed to doing quality work?
10. Do I have a best friend at work?
11. In the last six months, have I talked with someone about my progress?
12. At work, have I had opportunities to learn and grow?

Managers: Focus First On The Initial Six Questions

For example, it doesn't matter if you're helping develop your employees (question 12), if they don't know what's expected of them at work or don't have an opportunity to do what they do well (questions 1 and 3).

How We Created Sales Machine Alignment Through Salesforce.com's V2MOM Planning Process

One of Marc Benioff's key business practices that helped Salesforce.com grow to more than $1 billion in revenue in less than 10 years was the V2MOM planning process.

Marc Benioff came up with a plan to set the company's vision and align all of its people and teams in the execution of the vision. V2MOM stands for Vision, Values, Methods, Obstacles, and Metrics.

The V2MOM process helped the company (and the teams and people in it) lay out a vision, prioritize the most effective methods to achieve that vision, anticipate problems ahead of time, and understand how they would measure success. This was done at every level in the company: by the company as a whole, by teams, and also by each individual (i.e., I created a personal Aaron Ross V2MOM).

This creates alignment up and down the organization, from the CEO down to individual salespeople and support organizations.

We took the V2MOM process very seriously. The executive team alone spent 80-100 hours just in creating it at the CEO level. When I led my sales team, it took about 10-15 hours as a group to create the team version and then about 2-4 hours per individual for their personal versions.

It was well worth the investment.

Below are examples of the five principles of the V2MOM process at each level, so that you can learn from this to try it on your own:

1. VISION: What's The Big Picture?

What is your vision for the next 12 months?

- *Corporate:* "Double our enthusiastic and wildly successful global customer and partner community through flawless execution of our proven model."

- *Team (my sales team):* "Make a difference in the success of our team and company by being the best in the world at generating new business, through constant innovation and the sharing of our expertise."

- *Individual (from my personal V2MOM):* "Manage team members as a leader who will be remembered 10 years from now as their best ever."

2. VALUES: Top General Priorities?

What are the top three business values most important to keep in mind while working toward that vision?

- *Corporate:* "Customer Trust" — this was a top value during a year that Salesforce.com had recurring uptime and technology problems that were damaging trust with customers and partners — "Flawless Execution and Customer Success."

- *Team:* "Persistency. Efficiency. Success." Each can have multiple meanings. "Success" meant success of each individual on my team, of the sales team, of our prospects and customers, and anyone we came in contact with inside and outside of the company.

- *Individual:* "Hands-on Leadership. Watertight Execution. Practical Innovation."

3. METHODS: How Will It Happen?

What are the actual things you will do to hit your goals? What will you create? Rather than vague generalities, be as specific and clear as you can.

- *Corporate:* "Increase adoption through sales, service, and partner effectiveness by..." including more detailed specifics about programs and practices to clarify what this actually means.

- *Team:* "Don't take 'NO' until you get to the VP Sales." While it might seem obvious to have this as a sales tactic, I found that new salespeople gave up too easily when they received "no" from someone like the VP Marketing. It was so important to reinforce this practice of never giving up at an ideal prospect that we made it a V2MOM Method.

- *Individual:* "Lead from the trenches." I never asked people to do something I wouldn't do. I kept as close to them as possible and involved them in my own world as much as I could.

- *2nd personal example*: "A successful team is made up of successful individuals…" which meant I cultivated the mindset that I worked for them, rather than that they worked for me. By focusing on making every individual successful, the team succeeded.

4. OBSTACLES: What Is Or Could Be In The Way?

Identify landmines ahead of time to plan for and avoid.

- *Corporate*: "IT and corporate fear of having data outside the firewall."

- *Team*: "It's 'easier' to work harder than to work smarter." Putting in longer and longer hours is a crutch for people who don't know how to redesign their work or process to make it easier to get results. In our culture, it's easy to backslide into two habits to solve problems: "throw hours at it" and "throw money at it."

- *Individual*: "Size of team heading to 17 direct reports." The number of my direct reports was a challenge. When a team is growing, people need more attention and coaching. I found it very difficult to give each person the individual coaching and attention they needed once the team grew past 10 people. It was this kind of growth that kept me pushing the boundaries of creating self-managing systems, to find ways for peers to help and coach each other.

5. METRICS: How Will You Measure Success?

- *Corporate*: Revenue, adoption rates, etc.

- *Team*: We never measured daily dials or calls. Our method focused more on a series of results-based metrics such as Conversations Per Day, Qualified Opportunities Per Month, New Pipeline Per Month, and Total Closed Bookings.

- *Individual*: I had some key life- and Salesforce.com-related career goals here, such as "Make $170,000+ per year starting next year"; "Gain Asia and EMEA operating experience"; and "Complete Hawaii Half-Ironman in June 2005."

Three Ways To Inspire And Improve The Sales Organization

1. Include Salespeople In The Planning Of New Programs

Start by asking the sales organization about how they want to have their voices included in the business. What would they change? What would they do if they managed it?

Just as getting customer insight is important early in the product design process, you can save yourself a lot of frustration and get a much better "sales product" by including salespeople early in the design process.

You don't have to mandate feedback or ideas, just ask for volunteers. People don't necessarily want to contribute, but they do want the choice of being able to contribute.

There will be a reasonable number of people who want to actively help, either by offering ideas or in actually driving the process, so try letting them.

2. Beta Test New Sales Programs

Draft your program or rule, and then submit it to groups for feedback. Beta test it. Catch bugs or design issues early, before it's released to everyone.

Yes, this means you'll need to plan next year's territories and comp plans BEFORE the end of this year (shocking, I know!)

3. Survey Satisfaction

How satisfied are your salespeople with the support they get and their environment? What tools or parts of the environment are frustrating?

You can do this by walking the halls, posing the question in sales meetings, or using a simple service like www.surveymonkey.com.

It takes some work and creative thinking, but involving the sales force in the design of its own products will raise morale and engagement and improve their sales tools, both of which lead to more results.

Try this out with your sales organization, and then move to practicing it across the company.

Why Do Salespeople Resist Following Directions?

Executives from every company bemoan how their salespeople (and all other kinds of employees) don't follow processes, programs or directions. If all the programs, tools, and rules that you've created actually helped salespeople sell more, and had been communicated effectively, wouldn't salespeople be adopting more of them? So why don't they?

I'm going to use sales as the specific function and example for how to help employees get things done in a way that you see is beneficial to the company, such as following a sales process, but you can apply the principles anywhere in your organization.

The conventional sales management model is about telling people what to do and having them obey. Every sales executive and manager gets frustrated with salespeople not doing as they're told: "They don't use the sales force automation system... They don't make enough calls... They don't sell to value... They don't understand their compensation plan… Our training session attendance is poor... They don't forecast...".

One option is to bang your head against the wall as much as you can, trying to force or coerce salespeople into doing things. However, it's a very painful and frustrating way to try to drive behavior — for both sides.

And it doesn't even work very well anymore "with these uppity, demanding employees we have now who don't want to be ordered what to do and how to do it!"

Why:

1. People hate to be told what to do; thus coercion naturally creates resistance.

How do you feel when someone tells you to do something? (Rather than explaining why something's important and then asking for your teamwork or help.) Do you want to comply, or do you purposely want to not do it just to show them they can't tell you what to do?

2. It's a quick fix, not a solution.

Coercion is an attempt to find a shortcut around better user design. Great design is hard and takes time, and in our "urgency addicted" culture, we

172

tend to think, "How can we get this done now? How can we roll this out now?" (This is especially in sales, where there's always pressure for immediate results!)

3. You're going to lose the complexity battle.

All the sales programs, tools, plans, and rules only seem to get more complicated and grow over time. At some point, the complexity crosses an inflection point from "useful" to "hairball."

It's challenging balancing the values of more features and usability.

The best way to fight this battle is to improve how you choose and launch your internal processes, tools and programs. Involve your people! For example, even include salespeople in the process of updating a comp plan.

This doesn't work unless you take listening seriously. If you give lip service to listening and adopting feedback, nothing will change. Worse, should you ask for input and not institute any of it, you risk leaving your staff feeling undervalued which leads to morale issues, lowered productivity, and stressed staff.

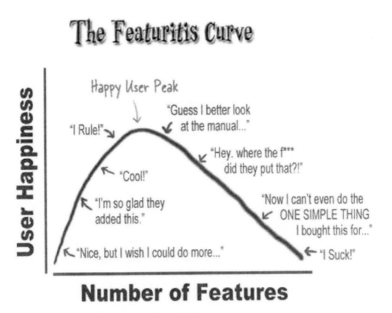

Source: the "Creating Passionate Users" blog

Your people aren't lazy, stubborn, or process-averse. *They are just averse to complicated processes that don't make sense to them, weren't explained properly, or don't help them.* In fact, they love intuitive processes and tools that help them sell more.

So, this thing you want your salespeople to do, is it something that will truly help them, or is it more of an administration function for your own benefit? The latter is okay, but you need to explain *why* it is important to the salespeople before they will buy in. Use the word "because" a lot in your communications.

Salespeople are all very busy, with all kinds of demands competing for their attention, so they instinctively prioritize their time.

Unless the tool or idea given to them is intuitive, they'll dismiss spending the mental time and energy to figure it out, and aren't most of us the same way?

Engage Their Help To Better Serve Your People

First, start learning how to earn, rather than demand, their attention. Instead of trying to push mandates or arbitrary programs onto salespeople, try a different approach: consider how you market to customers.

You earn the business and attention of customers. What if you tried thinking of salespeople as customers or users, and your tools, sales environment, and programs are the "products"?

Can you force your customers to do things? No. You have to design a product or service that they appreciate and that improves their business. In doing so, you earn the business and attention of your customers. The same can be done for your internal "customer" – your salespeople.

Consider what could happen if you made your sales organization "salesperson-centric"?

By the way, if you're having customer and marketing problems, part of it could be a reflection of what's not working with your internal marketing and servicing of your own employees.

Consider what could happen if you made your sales organization "salesperson-centric"? Since they're the ones actually working with customers and selling stuff, that can only be a good thing.

If you were to focus (with your employees as you do your customers) on usability and ROI — in this case, "return on salesperson's time" — how would you redesign your sales environment, organization, and tools?

Can you make whatever you want salespeople to spend time on as valuable to them as calling a prospect or customer?

Involve the sales teams in the identification, selection and design of initiatives, so they can feel like owners, get their input in early and become champions once it's ready to roll-out.

How To Design Self-Managing Teams And Processes

Ready to start shifting your teams toward more self-management?

Let's assume you have gone through at least the "Vision" portion of V2MOM or your own planning process, and your team has created a vision that includes a full or partial method of turning your employees into mini-CEOs with more self-managing systems.

The employees buy in because they want more control over their work, and they desire to become self-managing – even to the level of the janitor picking his own hours to come in and clean.

I recommend doing the following process with a single team first – such as a sales team – to find out what works for your culture, before moving on to other teams. Patiently and persistently keep at the goal of shifting the culture and team toward the common vision. Be prepared for it to take longer than you think, because you are dealing with changing habits – and habits don't like to change. Start by asking these two questions:

1. How would the team operate if the manager disappeared tomorrow?

2. What would have to happen for the team not to just continue operating at its current level, but actually to improve its results?

For example, here are some common key responsibilities of a VP Sales:

- Goal setting and achievement
- Personal involvement in big deals
- Culture
- Compensation – designing, calculating, reporting
- Talent – structuring roles, hiring, firing
- Coaching
- Analysis and reporting
- Budgeting / expenditures
- Process design and improvement

Take your list, starting at the top, and brainstorm your way down, point by point. For example, how would "Goal Setting and Achievement" work if the VP Sales disappeared tomorrow and wasn't replaced?

If you get stuck or feel like you want to cheat and pretend only one person can be the owner of that point, remember what Charles de Gaulle said: "The graveyards are full of indispensable men."

As you finish going through the list, a vision will shape as to how the team can self-manage itself. Don't try to implement every point on your list at once. Select a few (two or three) of the points that are the most important and easiest to implement, before moving on to the other points. Build some momentum with initial successes.

What's In It For The VP Sales (Or Any Manager)?

If you start giving away all the responsibilities and power of a manager, won't they feel threatened that you won't need them? No!

The more a sales team can manage itself, the more the VP Sales can focus on developing the "important, not urgent" aspects of the team, such as talent, culture and vision, rather than fighting fires or spending time on daily, "unimportant but urgent" tasks.

Even better, by freeing up their own time and energy, the VP Sales (and other executives) can take on more of your (the CEO's) responsibilities, and this allows you freedom and energy for even bigger things yourself!

See how this works? You get what you give. Create more freedom and upside for your people, and you'll get it in turn.

When Distributing Responsibilities, Begin With Elimination

As you work through your list of responsibilities and tasks, it's a perfect opportunity to use the 80/20 rule to clear out non-essential tasks. Rather than distributing 100% of the work of the manager, divide the work into two parts: 1) the 20% that is the most important to keep within the team or company, and 2) the 80% that can be eliminated, automated, or outsourced.

You can do this with two columns on a whiteboard: "Important 20%" and "Other 80%." In the 80% column, how can you first eliminate as much as possible?

Work through the responsibilities this way:

1. What can you Eliminate?
2. What can be Automated?
3. What can you Outsource?
4. Finally, Delegate or Distribute what is left.

For functions that can't be eliminated, how can you use the core CEOFlow values of Transparency and Trust to eliminate 80% of the reporting, monitoring, checking and auditing? (You can see more examples in my book *CEOFlow: How to Turn Your Employees Into Mini-CEO's* in the chapter on "The Power Of Transparency.")

For example, rather than having a process to pre-approve expenditures, try eliminating the approval process entirely, and transparently publish everyone's expense reports or team expenditures against budgets.

In that kind of expenditures system, create a process in which individuals must seek advice from others before spending money. It could be a process in which a peer, not a manager, must approve the expenditure. Peer review and transparency are a much more powerful and productive combination than administrative rules and regulations.

Then after eliminating and reducing as much as possible, go through and map out what you can automate or outsource, in ways that will both free your time and improve results.

After you've created plans for eliminating, automating, and outsourcing as much as possible, move on to delegating.

Distributing Management Through Sub-Teams And Team Leads

I will use a couple of terms here: (1) "Team Lead" and (2) "[Specific Function]" Lead, like "Training Program Lead."

When a group grows past 8-10 people, it is easy to begin losing that intimate, small team feel. People start feeling lost in a crowd – or worse, that they can hide.

When my sales team grew to 15 direct reports, well past my ability to give each person the amount of attention they deserved, I divided the team into three sub-teams of 5 people.

Each sub-team then selected their own "team lead," like a squad leader, who would best support them in their personal sales success.

These team leads were not managers but salespeople with extra responsibilities, there to ensure their sub-team functioned smoothly. They were my mini-CEOs that took over my daily and (to me) lower-value tasks like compensation reports (which were high-value to them, because they were learning and developing). While I often didn't have people on my team for more than 8 months (because we were growing so fast, and I kept promoting people), I would recommend you make team lead roles rotating positions, say every three-to-six months, so different people can develop and practice leadership skills.

Creating Sub-Teams Without Single Team Leads

Another way to create self-managing teams – rather than having any sort of team leads at all – is to spread responsibilities across the team by creating functional leads: "Goals Setting Lead," "New Hires Lead," "Education Lead," "Coaching System Lead," "Recruiting Lead," etc. You can rotate these roles every few months. Part of the responsibilities of an outgoing Lead is always to train the incoming Lead.

A functional lead doesn't have to be the one doing all the work. They are only responsible for it getting done, whether or not they do it.

A "Research Lead" could be responsible for managing an outsourced firm that is doing the actual research. A "Sales Hiring Lead" could be responsible for organizing the hiring process and making sure the interviews get done, without actually doing any interviews themselves.

A Team Leads Example

When you have a function that does need internal ownership by someone (like coaching of new hires), select a single person to be responsible for it – no committees. Make them a mini-CEO of that function.

Whether or not that person does the actual work isn't important. What is important is they are responsible for it getting done – and better than before.

For example, before I created my team leads and sub-teams system, I spent at least half of my time coaching and training new hires. As the team grew,

I wasn't able to give them and the veteran sales reps the time and attention they all deserved. When we moved to a team leads and sub-teams system, my sales team leads assumed 80%+ of the first few weeks of training and coaching for any new hire that entered their own sub-team. Each team lead ensured that the new hire ramped up on time over the first six weeks. I was free to coach the veterans on even more advanced sales skills.

Everybody won: new hires got more training and attention, veterans got more attention from me, and I could spend my own time on higher value work (such as coaching veterans on their career path instead of teaching new hires how to use Salesforce.com).

The team leads didn't do all of the coaching themselves; they were responsible for ensuring a new hire on their sub-team was trained and coached. After that I would then come in and spend more time with them, when they were ready for more advanced one-on-one coaching.

To align their goals with the goals of their sub-team, 20% of a team lead's goals and compensation depended on the whole sub-team's results. This 20% was extra compensation for taking on the responsibility of being a team lead.

The other 80% of a team lead's compensation depended on their individual sales performance.

Some of the other functions that the sub-teams and team leads owned included:

- Quality control of the work produced (we had an audit process to verify sales results and deals before approving them as commissionable).
- Small incentive/marketing budgets for their sub-team.
- Fun activities for their sub-team.
- Interviewing and training of new hires in their sub-team.
- Peer reviews of each other.
- Monthly achievement of sub-team sales goals.

I focused much of my time on coaching the team leads – training the trainers. As part of that, I still walked around and talked and sat with everyone, including new hires. Staying connected to the trenches gave me more insight into how to better help the team leads and improve our systems.

How To Distribute Responsibilities

You need to distribute responsibilities throughout the team (or to outside the team) in ways that don't add a lot of extra work; hence the importance of elimination, automation and outsourcing before delegation.

By distributing responsibilities to the employees touching customers, the ones closest to the action, you can get better quality work and results. They will also learn much more about the business and what it takes to succeed as mini-CEOs.

Here are some examples of distributing some common VP Sales responsibilities:

Goal Setting:

What conditions would have to exist for the team to be able to set and achieve its own goals better than before?

- 80/20 rule: How much of the goals-setting process isn't that important? Do you really need to set and track 15 goals? What are the 20% of the goals that matter the most?
- What if you have a "Goals Setting Lead" on the team to be the point person to manage the process, both within the team and with the CEO?
- Do you need a separate "Quota Beating Lead" to monitor and report on the teams overall progress each month, and flag areas of concern?

Senior Help On Big Deals:

If you have to throw your VP Sales (or yourself) at every big deal, you don't have a scalable sales process, and that one person will always be a bottleneck. In fact, any time a single person is a bottleneck to any process, your growth is capped. What conditions would have to exist for 80% of your current big deals to close without help from the VP Sales or CEO?

- Can you enhance your sales process or product to reduce the need for VP Sales involvement? To make deals easier to win without as much help?
- Which other senior executives can be placed "on call" to step into big deals?

- Could customers who love you contribute some of their time to helping you? (Yes, this can happen, especially if you have a special privileges program for them.)

Sales Reporting And Analysis:

What conditions would have to exist for the team and executives to get all the reports and analysis they need with the click of a button?

- By publishing the sales results in real-time, such as with an application like Salesforce.com, can you eliminate the need for someone to do reporting altogether?

- Be aware of data-addiction: Which reports are nice-to-have versus need-to-have? It is common for executives and board members who ask for reports to forget that many take considerable time and energy to produce, and that time isn't free because it takes people away from the business. Rather than blindly producing reports, ask them their business goal for the report. Maybe they need something other than what they want. Help executives understand the cost of the reports they want, so they can prioritize their requests.

- How can you redesign your reports to be more useful? Reports are often created just because someone wants it without a clear idea of its purpose. Ask, "What decision will this report help you make better? What is the goal of this report?" If a report doesn't help you prioritize your energies or make better decisions, something's wrong with it.

Culture:

A lot of companies like to talk about culture, but then actually do little about it. Often it's little more than another coercion tool foisted on employees to "Get your head in the game" and "Be a part of the team." How much do you do to encourage and develop a positive culture that attracts and supports great people? What conditions would have to exist for the culture to identify and practice its key values? Example:

- If having fun is important to your culture (and it better be!), the team could have a Fun Lead who would be accountable for the team having fun each week. No, "accountable fun" is not an oxymoron. When people are busy, it's easy to forget to have fun.

- Again, that person may or may not be the person organizing events, instigating practical jokes, or starting impromptu office karaoke sessions – they only need to make sure it happens regularly.

Never Give Up

Why can it feel hard to develop self-managing people and teams? Assuming you have hired good people (which is frequently not the case), a main cause of failure is giving up too soon. This requires patience and practice.

For some of you, it might take six weeks to make a team self-managing. For others, it could be six years. But if you give up along the way, you for sure will never make it happen. Stay committed to it and never give up!

For more about "turning your employees into mini-CEOs", visit: www.CEOFlow.com.

Engage The Whole Team In Designing Their Compensation

Even though I retained some core responsibilities – comp plan design, V2MOM/vision planning, annual planning – I still gave everyone the option of getting involved in those functions, if they wanted to. Involving employees (or giving them the option of involvement) in the creation of everything is vital to inspiring them to care about the business as much as you do.

For example, at one point several sales team members were expressing frustration about the design of the compensation plan, which had three components:

- A fixed base salary,
- A variable commission based on how many qualified (and audited/confirmed) opportunities that person generated in a month, and
- A variable commission based on how much revenue had been sourced by that person.

The complaints were a little varied but ultimately came down to the fact that I hadn't taken enough time to educate some of the newer sales reps on why we had that system.

Rather than even telling them why it was designed that way, I instead set up a process to get the team's help to revisit and redesign the comp plan. Out of about 15 people at the time, 5 opted-in to help.

We had one main session to dig into the issue, to review the team's priorities and goals (identified through the V2MOM process), and to create a forum for them to share their ideas on how to better shape the comp plan to support the goals.

After a couple hours of discussion, which included revisiting even the basic assumptions surrounding how we measured performance and success, and if we should use different metrics, the team came to the conclusion that the current comp plan was the best one.

Rather than just telling them why the comp plan evolved into its current form, I led them through their own discovery process. They "got it" and the complaints stopped. Even better, they could be much more effective in teaching other team members or new hires about the comp plan so these frustrations didn't pop up again with the next generation of new team members. We ended up in the same place we began: the comp plan didn't change. One could feel like we wasted time, but I felt it was a fantastic use of time as a coaching exercise and as a way to increase trust and transparency in the team. The reps felt more connected to the team and the systems because they now understood more intimately where everything came from and why – they owned it.

My only disappointment was that I had hoped they would come up with something I had missed so we could improve the plan!

Transparent Compensation And Reporting

I had a convenient advantage that helped me transparently publish everyone's compensation on the team: they all were on the same basic plan structure (same base salary, same bonus and commission rates). No one had special deals even though some people had much more experience than others. Those with more experience or expectations could earn the extra compensation through higher results.

With transparency compensation, the whole team could see who earned the most and why – how their higher results translated directly into more money.

Publishing compensation also eliminated compensation and payroll errors, and reduced by 80% the amount of time I had to spend on tracking and reporting compensation. If you haven't tracked and reported on compensation, it's a pain. For a long time, we used spreadsheets at Salesforce.com to report commissionable results.

The secrecy model:

- Run the reports: What were each person's results?
- Prepare the report and calculate commissions.
- Cut the report into private reports for each person.
- Email or sit with each person to share results and ensure correctness.
- Fix the report as necessary.

- Combine all the results into one spreadsheet.
- Send to finance.

And that is when it works! If there is some issue in the report or with finance, the process gets into a painful circle of "fix-resend-check-fix-resend-check..." When the team grew past a handful of people, I started using transparency to eliminate 80% of this work and streamline the process.

I put all the sales results into a single spreadsheet, with the calculated commissions.

I then emailed the entire sheet to the whole team. Everyone could see everyone's results, and how they personally ranked.

Yes, everyone could see on our Salesforce.com dashboards how they ranked in numbers of opportunities or deals, but in the spreadsheet they could rank themselves by total compensation.

They could see exactly who was doing the best and thus whom they could model or go to for advice (we had a culture of helping each other succeed).

They could see if there were any problems with the report. They felt confident that they would get the right paycheck from finance, which is not true for many organizations – compensation payment issues are all-too common.

They could trust in the process and not worry about it, because we were open and transparent with it.

Ultimately, switching to this transparent process made comp reporting a snap for me and for them!

I never took it to the next level, which would have been to have someone volunteer to be the Comp Lead, to manage the reporting and processing for me. But that would have been an easy next step.

10 Ways To Improve Sales Force Automation Adoption

Sales Force Automation systems like Salesforce.com are ESSENTIAL tools; but like any tool, it's only as valuable as the proficiency with which it is used. As easy to use as Salesforce.com is – and other systems can be – many companies still struggle to get their people to use them.

Three Core Adoption Values

1. Executives must lead by example

Adoption starts with the CEO and executive team. As a rule of thumb, users will only adopt as far as their managers do, and managers will adopt only as far as the executives do.

2. Better design = better adoption

The easier you make it for people to adopt (cleaner interface, comprehensive training, initial handholding), the more they will.

3. Peer pressure and collaboration work

Starting with the executive team, everyone needs to expect your SFA system will be used. Ask, "Why isn't this in our sales system?" until you're sick of even hearing yourself. Bring meetings to a halt until the sales system is updated NOW.

10 Ways To Increase Adoption Of Your Sales Force Automation ("SFA") System

1. Set up a useful CEO/executive team dashboard, PLUS include a slot in the executive meeting to review the dashboard.
2. Clean up your SFA clutter to improve usability.
3. Make compensation dependent on accurate reports in your system.
4. Clearly communicate why SFA adoption matters.
5. Customize the user interface for your people by role.
6. Start training and creating expectations Day One with new hires.

7. Make adoption a part of sales culture and peer pressure.

8. Take an online training class for your sales force automation system.

9. Hire an experienced SFA user of your system to do one-on-one training sessions with your people.

10. Evaluate a mobile smartphone version of your SFA system.

Explanations

1. Set up a useful CEO/executive team dashboard, PLUS include a slot in the executive meeting to review the dashboard.

What metrics are currently tracked in weekly executive meetings? Translate these out of Excel and into a SFA dashboard (where possible), using the dashboard as the basis of that part of the meeting. No exceptions. This will create a top-down effect that will greatly help in inspiring adoption!

Start simple, with a single first dashboard and only the top 8-10 metrics the team cares about. Examples: Closed sales quarter to date, Open deals slated to close this quarter, Number of leads qualified this month, Pipeline created this month, Results per vertical, etc.

2. Clean up your SFA clutter to improve usability.

Stop trying to track EVERYTHING. The easier your SFA system is to use, the more people will use it. Get rid of the clutter, mostly by hiding things people don't use and keeping labels intuitive:

- Hide unused tabs.
- Hide or remove unused data fields.
- Use simple, common sense names for custom fields.

3. Make compensation dependent on reports in your SFA system.

Don't pay people if the sales opportunity or customer isn't in your SFA system, or if it's not filled out to pre-defined standards. You'll be amazed at how quickly opportunities move into your SFA system!

4. Clearly communicate why SFA adoption matters.

Studies have shown that when you clearly communicate why you want something, people are much more likely to cooperate. You won't get much

Without data in your SFA system, the executive team must either navigate blindly or extract data manually...

cooperation from salespeople if they feel like you only want them to use the SFA because you want to keep tabs on them. But if they know why it's good business for them to use it, they will...

Without data in your SFA system, the executive team must either navigate blindly or extract data manually from people, hurting the sales team in either case.

Sales reps will waste time as teammates (pre-sales, inside sales) struggle or make mistakes because of inaccurate or incomplete views of accounts and their status.

Customers will be more likely to receive poor service, as customer support won't have a clear picture of what's going on with the account.

5. Customize the user interface for your people by role.

Find out what sales reps need from the SFA, and how they could benefit - then configure a specific user interface for them that excludes anything irrelevant and distracting.

6. Start training and creating expectations Day One with new hires.

Make a first impression and reinforce the idea that everything should and does live in the SFA. Start them with good habits.

7. Make it a part of sales culture and peer pressure.

"If it's not in the SFA system, it doesn't exist." If management holds a high standard of expectations and doesn't cheat, reps will improve.

Example: On a pipeline call, if a rep hasn't entered or updated a deal, make the team wait while they update it in real-time (assuming they're at a computer).

Again, don't pay people for deals that are not in the system.

8. Take an online SFA training class.

Whatever system you have, there are different kinds of classes – take them! While in a perfect world you could use a system just by looking at it and it would be totally intuitive, until Apple gets into this market, you will have to take training.

9. Have experienced SFA users do one-on-one training sessions.

I've found that many users of SFA systems are, for the most part, just intimidated by a "new system." Sitting down with them for a couple of half-hour sessions, to show them just a few useful tips, is enough to get them over the main first hump.

10. Evaluate a mobile smartphone version of your SFA system.

Would SFA on Blackberries/iPhones make it more accessible? Especially for salespeople on the road who have little time to update things on a laptop, this can be an easy way to give them access to make small, yet important, updates or to access data in the system from anyplace at anytime.

Remember, it's not just the responsibility of the software you choose to make you successful, or the sales reps themselves.

The CEO bears the most responsibility here in also using it and staying committed to doing whatever it takes to help the company embrace it and use it effectively.

Sell - don't command - people on the value and vision of what it will be like to have it embraced!

Who's Responsibility Is Adoption?

Ultimately, it's not the responsibility of the software you choose to make you successful.

It's also not the sales reps' responsibility or sales managers, although they of course are very important to adoption.

Who bears the ultimate responsibility for successfully deploying and adopting a sales system?

The CEO (or business division leader).

The teams will follow the CEOs lead: if you use your sales system, the company will. If you don't use it, they won't. You must lead by example.

Sell - don't command - people on the value and vision of what it will be like to have your system embraced!

190

11

Next Steps and Resources

Where do you go from here?

Where Will You Go From Here?

If you've read through this book and checked out the extra resources on PredictableRevenue.com, you will have no shortage of ideas, questions and plans.

So now, what are you going to DO about it? What steps will you take?

I've found that it's challenging to bring much new information into a company at any one time, that BABY STEPS work. Don't be afraid to take small steps sometimes. Just don't stop taking them. Be unstoppable.

While the Cold Calling 2.0 process is simple, sticking to it and ingraining it in your culture may not be. Change is hard for people and companies.

Commitment Is The Key:

"Until one is committed, there is hesitancy, the chance to draw back-- Concerning all acts of initiative (and creation), there is one elementary truth that ignorance of which kills countless ideas and splendid plans: that the moment one definitely commits oneself, then Providence moves too. All sorts of things occur to help one that would never otherwise have occurred. A whole stream of events issues from the decision, raising in one's favor all manner of unforeseen incidents and meetings and material assistance, which no man could have dreamed would have come his way. Whatever you can do, or dream you can do, begin it. Boldness has genius, power, and magic in it. Begin it now." - Goethe

The following pages have some recommendations for further things to think about as well as suggestions for other teachers and consultants to investigate.

Follow These People

The following are a mix of consultants, authors, bloggers and entrepreneurs that I recommend you follow or reach out to for help with your own sales, marketing and lead generation challenges:

- Brian Carroll: www.StartWithaLead.com
- Tom Batchelder: www.Perficency.com
- Jon Miller: www.Marketo.com/blog
- Craig Rosenberg: www.Funnelholic.com
- Phoneworks: www.PhoneWorks.com
- Anneke Seley and Brent Holloway: www.Sales20Book.com
- Josiane Feigon: www.Tele-Smart.com/blog
- Jep Castelein: www.LeadSloth.com
- Eliot Burdett: www.PeakSalesRecruiting.com
- Kevin Gaither: www.InsideSalesRecruiting.com
- Daniel Zamudio: www.Playboox.com
- Thousands of experts: www.Focus.com

Products To Watch

Many companies are building interesting things in the sales and lead generation markets. Here are a handful of particularly interesting ones.

- ConnectAndSell.com: Delivers live conversations on demand.
- SalesCrunch.com: Online sales presentations and much more.
- InsideView.com: Sales intelligence & productivity.
- Marketo.com: Marketing automation & revenue performance.
- XactlyCorp.com: Sales compensation management.
- EchoSign.com: Online document signing.
- VisualizeROI.com: Interactive ROI tool for selling & leadgen.

Sales Training & Education Services

Our sales training business' mission is to help you grow faster with more peace of mind and predictability rather than more hard work. Our workshops and classes take the ideas of the book and build on them with tools, templates, step-by-step training videos, examples and live training and coaching.

We work with clients that value their people, rather than treating them like disposable resources. The quality of your people and their training is what will make or break you. We believe the better you treat and train your people, the faster and easier your growth will be. The best people - yes, even salespeople - value learning and career development over money.

Predictable Revenue education helps you:

- Multiply your growth by walking you through *exactly* how to build an outbound sales function ("Cold Calling 2.0") that generates a predictable monthly flow of highly qualified leads.
- Hire, develop, and retain great salespeople.
- Connect with like-minded peers who are going through similar challenges, so that you can learn from each other.
- Create "CEOFlow": a happy, autonomous workforce by turning your employees into mini-CEOs.

Contact Us Or Find Free Training Resouces

www.PredictableRevenue.com

Unique Genius: Make Money Through Enjoyment

In addition to money, don't you - and more people around you than ever - also want *meaningful* work, to do something that matters?

You - like everyone - are unique in your own special way. You have a purpose in life, and can discover it. You can mash up all your varied interests, passions and ideas into a fulfilling, successful business.

When you are living aligned with your unique purpose, competition doesn't exist. Your compeititors transform into collaborators.

You Can Make As Much Money As You Want, Doing What You Love

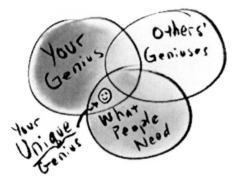

You can create a successful job or business around values such as compassion, integrity, play, honor, service and authenticity. You can love your days and *feel like you matter*, but you can make a great living from it without having to sacrifice quality time with your family and friends..

Start A Fulfilling, Freeing Business

Find our educational videos at: www.UniqueGenius.com

About The Authors

Aaron Ross

Aaron Ross is the founder of PebbleStorm, and is helping 100 million people "make money through enjoyment" by combining money and happiness.

A keystone program of PebbleStorm is the Unique Genius programs, which help people discover their purpose, values and passions and then turn them into fulfilling, fun, freeing work.

You can download a free Unique Genius ebook, "You Can Make As Much Money As You Want, Doing What You Love," at: www.PebbleStorm.com/manifesto

Aaron is the author of *CEOFlow: Turn Your Employees Into Mini-CEOs*, which teaches leaders to free up their own time and energy by creating a culture of self-managing systems in which employees help run the business like high-level executives.

Aaron Ross and Marylou Tyler co-founded Predictable Revenue, Inc. which helps companies generate as many highly qualified sales opportunities as they want, creating a very predictable source of revenue.

Before PebbleStorm, Aaron Ross was EIR (Entrepreneur-in-Residence) at Alloy Ventures, a $1 billion venture capital firm. Prior to Alloy, Aaron created a revolutionary sales lead generation process at Salesforce.com that helped increase recurring revenues by $100 million.

Aaron was CEO of LeaseExchange (now eLease.com), an online equipment leasing marketplace.

He has been featured in *Time, Business Week* and *The Red Herring*.

Aaron graduated from Stanford University with a degree in Environmental Civil Engineering. He is an Ironman triathlete, graduate of the Boulder Outdoor Survival School and an avid motorcycle rider (www.MotoCEOs. com).

Marylou Tyler

Marylou Tyler, CEO of Predictable Revenue, Inc., is a serial entrepreneur and "Chief Conversation Starter." She loves to help companies find effective, repeatable ways to sell products and services in the digital age.

Marylou's sales passion is teaching sales professionals how to eliminate fear and rejection by using simple, friendly and predictable techniques at the most critical point in the sales cycle – finding and having the initial conversation.

Before cofounding Predictable Revenue, Inc., Marylou founded Telegenik Communications, a consultancy firm that helped clients grow sales and specialized in surveying customer and market needs for more than a decade.

While at Telegenik, Marylou discovered Aaron Ross' Predictable Revenue processes and implemented them for an enterprise software client, tripling their pipeline results in 90 days. Her efforts caught the attention of Aaron Ross (*She is a superstar, and is better at this than me!* - Aaron) and together they formed Predictable Revenue, Inc.

In addition to being a teacher, coach and author, Marylou is a mother of two, triathlete, philanthropist and volunteers at a non-profit that helps foster shelter dogs. Marylou is a Californian currently residing in Des Moines, IA.

CPSIA information can be obtained at www.ICGtesting.com
Printed in the USA
BVOW010339160812

297930BV00003B/136/P